Feeding your vegan infant - with confidence

A practical guide from pre-conception through to pre-school

by Sandra Hood, Vegan Dietitian
with contributions from Louise Blake, Vegan Mother

First published September 2005

ISBN 0-907337-29-5

Published by The Vegan Society
Donald Watson House,
7 Battle Road,
St Leonards-on-Sea,
East Sussex TN37 7AA,
United Kingdom.
www.vegansociety.com

Design: Doughnut Design

Illustrations: Juliet Breese

Cover photo: Corin Jeavons

Printed in England by Biddles Ltd, King's Lynn,
www.biddles.co.uk

Acknowledgements

Thank you to everyone who contributed to this book. I would particularly like to thank the late Arthur Ling who provided the inspiration to write. The time and patience afforded to me by Paul and Galina Appleby, Amy Austin, Louise Blake, Julie Charman, Vanessa Clarke and Stephen Walsh, Brenda Davis, Nicole Davis, Sue Hardy, Reed Mangels, Jerry Nash, Amanda Rofe, my sister Alison Salmon, Lynn Sawyer, Catriona Toms and Zoue Lloyd-Wright is much appreciated.

Deepest appreciation also to the parents for their wise words and to the children whose lovely photos are a testimony to the benefits of a vegan diet: Keith and his mother Sue Wilson; Sorcha, Finn and Rory and mother Anne Cooper; Otis and Finton and parents Joanna and Jonathan Eatwell-Hurst; Romy and parents Hazel and Colin Smithson; Mia and Matilda and parents Louise and Simon Blake; David and father Harry Mather; Carlin and mother Audrey Bowman; Mair and mother Gwen Perkins; Adam and Amber and parents Sharon and Paul Cook; Tyra and Keisha and mother Jayne Hilaire; Tom and Peter and parents John and Jessica Wintrip; Matthew and Alice and mother Lisa Baxter; Joe, Bridie and Natasha and parents Alison and Iain Salmon.

Vision

2004 marked the vision that Donald Watson showed 60 years ago in creating the Vegan Society. Now Sandra carries forward this vision in presenting this book with it being the first ever on weaning vegan infants on an exclusively vegan diet.

Sandra takes parents step by step through every stage of an infant's life. This enables parents and in certain cases health professionals to realize how unwise it is to generalize and how important it is to treat infants as individuals who need to be given individual attention.

During the past 60 years there have been hundreds of cookery books published but Sandra has shown commendable vision in dealing for the first time ever with vegan upbringing for which there is a tremendous need for clear parental guidance. This book should be in every vegan home; the future generation and the benefits of the vegan diet are central to its message. Congratulations Sandra on your great vision.

Arthur Ling 1919 -2005
Former patron of the Vegan Society and Managing Director of Plamil Foods. Editor of *Vegan Infant Case Histories 1971-2000*.

Contents

Introduction

All parents want to give their child the best start in life and feeding your child a nourishing diet is an essential part of this. To many parents, feeding cow's milk and other dairy products to children is among the most natural and healthful acts in the world. However, with the increase in obesity and other childhood complaints such as asthma, eczema, ear infections and most recently, childhood diabetes, some doctors and health professionals are questioning the role that dairy products play in our children's diet. Clinical evidence suggests that these foods are not natural foods for children (or adults!) and children do not need to drink the milk of cows to grow fit and healthy [1]. All life ultimately depends on plants so to say that animal products are an essential part of life has been conclusively proved wrong. Indeed, drinking cow's milk is not recommended by the Department of Health for a child under 12 months of age [2]. A vegan diet can provide all the nutrients for good health, growth and development and may protect against many chronic diseases that afflict the western world. The aim of this book is to provide practical advice on how and what to feed your child and to reassure parents that bringing their children up on a vegan, cruelty free diet benefits the growing child, animals and the environment.

Raising a child as a vegan also enables parents or carers to discuss with a young one where food comes from, why they are being raised vegan and consequently instilling an appreciation and respect for food as well as embracing cooking and eating as happy experiences. *'Feeding your vegan infant - with confidence'* will help you do this.

What is a vegan diet?

A diet that excludes any food that comes from animals. This includes **milk** and **dairy products, eggs** and **honey.** Many vegans do not wear animal products, including leather, wool and silk. Vegans also strive to avoid using any products which contain animal ingredients, including cosmetics and household cleaning products.

WHY A VEGAN DIET?

There is no doubt that many chronic diseases of adulthood manifest themselves in childhood and the importance of early nutrition to prevent disease in later life is now generally accepted [3,4,5,6,7,8]. Studies to date suggest that vegans may be less likely to suffer from "common diseases of affluence" such as obesity, diabetes, cardiovascular disease, high blood pressure, heart disease and cancer [9,10]. In the UK obesity is increasing among school aged children with fat and sugar intakes higher than the Department of Health recommendations [11,12]. In contrast, vegan children have generally been found to be lighter in weight than their peers, consume more fruit and vegetables, and have a low level of dental caries [13]. The British Dietetic Association state that [vegan] diets "more closely approach key UK dietary recommendations than omnivorous diets" [14] and the American Dietetic Association stated that "appropriately planned vegan diets satisfy nutrient needs of infants, children and adolescents and promote normal growth" [13].

Not so long ago, vegetables, grains, beans and fruit were only viewed as accompaniments to meals but now these foods are accepted as the most important part of our diet. Indeed, only recently the USA recommended that children need to eat a minimum of five portions of fruits and vegetables daily and adults a minimum of seven to nine[15] (see pages 4-5 for portion guide). Nevertheless, various studies over the last few years have shown that, like adults, omnivore children are falling prey to the pitfalls of the Western diet. Recent studies have raised concerns about increasing obesity with pre-school children eating more processed foods than recommended and not enough fruit and the prevalence of anaemia and dental caries is a concern[11]. The UK is now the heaviest nation in Europe. The Food Standards Agency is to work with industry and government to improve the diet of young people in the UK following publication of a Government report in 2000. The report showed that the young people aged 4-18 years were eating large amounts of sugar, salt and saturated fat and not enough fruit and vegetables[12]. Whereas it has been shown that appropriately planned vegan diets are healthful, nutritionally adequate and that vegan children tend to have lower intakes of saturated fat and cholesterol than non-vegan children[16]. The vegan diet has the answer!

With increased interest in the vegan diet for reasons of health, economics, the environment and world hunger, it is important that a vegan diet is thoroughly understood. There are so many misconceptions about vegan diets and these need to be tackled. Hopefully this book will do so. Children who grow up getting their nutrition from plant foods potentially have a tremendous health advantage and are less likely to develop health problems as they grow up. The vegan diet is the diet of the twenty-first century and beyond!

VEGAN FOOD GUIDE
– the balance of good health

Over the years a number of food guides have been developed and in the USA a food pyramid is used (see overleaf).

Following trials, the UK opted for the Balance of Good Health[17], now adopted by the Food Standards Agency, which is flexible enough to be applicable to all age-groups from toddlers to elderly people. There are varying divisions on the plate, each representing one of five food groups to show the types and proportions of foods in a well balanced and healthy diet. On the whole, vegans tend to eat more healthily than the general population[14] and so have a head start. The plate model has been adapted for the vegan diet and is intended as a guide only. The ranges allow for differences in age, body size and activity levels.

USA FOOD PYRAMID

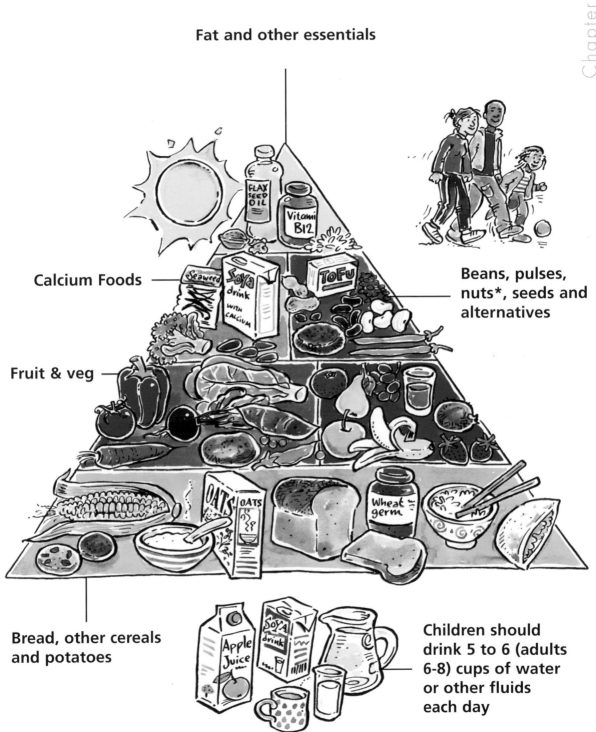

Fat and other essentials

Calcium Foods

Beans, pulses, nuts*, seeds and alternatives

Fruit & veg

Bread, other cereals and potatoes

Children should drink 5 to 6 (adults 6-8) cups of water or other fluids each day

*if there is a history of allergy, peanuts need to be avoided until 3 years of age

Based on the vegetarian food guide © 2000 by Vesanto Melina, Brenda Davis and David Brousseau

THE BALANCE OF GOOD HEALTH

Fruit & veg

Number of daily measures	What counts as a measure? (approximately 80g)
Five or more	2 tbspns vegetables Small salad Small glass (100 ml) fruit juice Piece of fresh fruit 2 tbspn stewed fruit

Beans, pulses, nuts* seeds & alternatives

Number of daily measures	What counts as a measure? (approximate measures)
Two or more servings	100g pulses/lentils (cooked) 100g tofu 50g tahini/nut butter 50g nuts/seeds 2 soya sausages/1 soya burger 300ml fortified non dairy milk

Bread, other cereals & potatoes

Number of daily measures	What counts as a measure? (approximate measures)
Four or more	3 tbs breakfast cereal 1 slice of bread/toast Bread bun/roll Small pitta bread/chapatti 3 crackers Small potato/sweet potato 1 tbspn rice 2 tbspns pasta

Calcium foods
(see page 56 for other sources of calcium)

Number of daily measures	What counts as a measure? (approximate measures)
Three or more	300 mls fortified non-dairy milk 25g tofu 50g nuts* eg almonds 40g (approx 3) dried figs

*peanuts need to be avoided until 3 years of age if there is a history of allergy

Fats & other essentials

Number of daily measures	What counts as a measure? (approximate measures)
Small amounts	**Omega-3 fatty acids**: Flaxseed oil (1 tspn); rapeseed oil (1 tbspn); walnuts (3 tbspns) **Vitamin B12** (3-10mcg daily) **Iodine**: sea vegetables, kelp tablets, Vecon (2-3 times per week)

The following gives further detail on the different food groups – try to include a variety of foods every day consisting of these different food groups:

- *Breads, other cereals and potatoes*
These foods should form the basis of meals and snacks. Choose from wholemeal or wholegrain but these should not be used exclusively for children with small appetites. A variety of different cereals and grains can be used.

- *Fruit and vegetables*
Aim for at least five portions of fruit and vegetables every day preferably including leafy dark green types. It may be necessary to peel fruit and vegetables for infants and young children so that not too much bulk is provided. Children's stomachs are small and can easily be filled up before they have had enough energy.

- *Calcium foods*
Many of these calcium containing foods duplicate those in the other sections of the plate model. Including a variety of these foods will ensure an adequate intake.

- *Beans, pulses, nuts, seeds and meat alternatives*
These foods are important for protein, vitamins and minerals. Buying tinned varieties of beans and pulses can save on cooking time but avoid the brands with added salt and sugar.

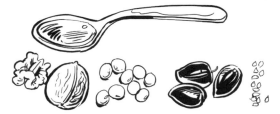

- *Fats, vitamin B12 and iodine*
Only small amounts of these foods are needed. Getting the right balance of essential fatty acids (EFAs) is important. Try to include a regular source of w-3 (omega-3) fatty acids found in rapeseed, flaxseed and walnut oil (see chapter 6 for more information on fatty acids). One teaspoon of flaxseed (linseed) oil or one tablespoon of rapeseed (canola) oil per day can help to achieve the right balance of essential fatty acids. Flax powder is now available and can be sprinkled on dishes. Olive oil is also a good choice as it is neither w-3 nor w-6 (omega 6) fatty acid and so does not further upset the ratio between these 2 families of fatty acids. Small amounts of added fats help children meet their needs for energy and essential fatty acids*.

*The general public is constantly encouraged to include fish in the diet, particularly oily varieties rich in w-3 fatty acids, for cardiovascular protection[18]. Some vegans have perhaps felt they are missing out health wise from not consuming fish. However, fish consumption does not reduce the risk of death from cardiovascular disease in low risk people and people with healthy lifestyles gain no additional protection from eating fish. Moreover, one teaspoon of flaxseed oil per day provides a similar amount of plant w-3s used in the heart protection study of 1994[18].

Include a reliable source of iodine eg seaweed, iodised salt, Vecon (yeast extract) or kelp containing supplements at least 2-3 times per week. There is iodine in vegetables and grains but amounts vary according to the iodine content of the soil and studies suggest a low iodine concentration in soil.

Include a daily source of vitamin B12 from fortified foods such as fortified non-dairy milks, fortified cereals and yeast extracts or consider taking a supplement (see page 17 for further details on this important vitamin).

Putting it into practice

So now you have a basic understanding on what makes up a balanced diet you are ready to embark on the exciting journey of preparing yourself and your baby for the best start in life!

References for Chapter 1

1 Mangels AR Messina V Melina V (2003) *Position of the American Dietetic Assocation and Dietitians of Canada: Vegetarian Diets* J Am Diet Assoc 103 748-65

2 MAFF (1997) *A guide for health professionals: Healthy diets for infants and young children* Ministry of Agriculture, Fisheries and Food

3 Barker DJP (1996) *The origins of coronary heart disease in early life in long-term consequences of early environment growth development and the Lifespan Developmental Perspectives* eds CJK Henry & SJ Ulijaszek Cambridge Cambridge Press

4 Chapin RE Robbins WA Schieve LA Sweeney AM Tabacova SA Tomashek KM (2004) *Off to a good start: the influence of pre- and periconceptional exposures, parental fertility and nutrition on children's health* Environmental Health Perspectives 112 1 69-78

5 Falkner B Sherif K Michel S Kushner H (2000) *Dietary nutrients and blood pressure in urban minority adolescents at risk for hypertension* Arch Pediatr Adolesc Med 154 918-922

6 Gillman MW (2002) *Epidemiological challenges in studying the fetal origins of adult chronic disease* Int J Epidemiol 31 294-299

7 Martin RM McCarthy A Smith GD Davies DP Ben-Shlomo Y (2003) *Infant nutrition and blood pressure in early adulthood: the Barry Caerphilly Growth study* Am J Clin Nutr Jun 77(6) 1489-97

8 McGill HC McMahan CA Herderick EE Malcom GT Tracy RE Strong JP (2000) *Origin of atherosclerosis in childhood and adolescence* Am J Clin Nutr 72 (suppl) 1307S-1315S

9 Appleby P Davey GK Key TJ (2002) *Hypertension and blood pressure among meat eaters fish eaters vegetarians and vegans in EPIC-Oxford* Public Health Nutrition 5(5) 645-654

10 Hubbard RW Mejia A Horning M (1994) *Potential of diet to alter disease processes* Nutr Research Vol 14 12 1853-1895

11 Power C Lake J Cole T (1997) *Body mass index and height from childhood to adulthood in the 1958 British birth cohort* Am J Clin Nutr 1997 66 1094-101

12 National Diet & Nutrition Survey (2000) *National Diet & Nutrition Survey: young people aged 4 to 18 years* The Stationary Office: London

13 Sanders TAB Manning J (1992) *The growth and development of vegan children* JH Nutr & Diet 5 11-21

14 Thomas B (2001) *Practical dietary advice for vegetarians* in Manual of Dietetic Practice pp309

15 Gottlieb S (2003) *Men should eat nine servings of fruit and vegetables a day* BMJ Vol 326 1003 15 March 2003

16 Dwyer JT Dietz WH Jr Andrews EM Suskind RM (1982) *Nutritional status of vegetarian children* Am J Clin Nutr Feb 35 (2) 204-16

17 Health Education Authority (1994) *The Balance of Good Health*. Introducing the National Food Guide London HEA

18 De Lorgeril M et al (1994) *Mediterranean alpha-linolenic acid-rich diet in secondary prevention of coronary heart disaese* The Lancet 343 1454-1459

Pre-Conceptional Nutrition
preparing for your baby - give your baby the best start in life

To maximise your chances of having a healthy baby, it is important for both parents to start getting the body into the best possible condition. It takes approximately six months for any lifestyle changes to have an effect on fertility. It is suggested that the developing embryo, the development of the foetus, the health of the infant, child and adolescent and the long term health of the adult may have its origins in the health of the egg and sperm.[1] If you produce healthy eggs and sperm, this can only be a bonus to the developing baby in handling the exposures of modern day life.

MALE NUTRITION
As discussed, the health of the child starts pre-conceptually, and at this stage the health status of the father is as important as the mother. There is undisputed evidence that men significantly effect the health of children through sperm[1]. Sperm is produced constantly in the testes and it takes three to four months for sperm to mature. The number and quality of sperm, and the health of the prostate gland (involved in semen production) are important in deciding how fertile a man is.

Medical conditions, eg diabetes mellitus, cystic fibrosis, kidney disease and long term stress, can affect sperm count so it is important to consult your specialist to ensure health status is optimum.

Since the 1940s sperm concentration has declined by 40% and the volume of sperm has declined by 20%[2]. Various suggestions have been made as to why this has occurred and diet remains top of the list[3]. Sperm are highly vulnerable to free radical and oxidative damage. Healthy sperm formation requires an adequate and ready supply of proper nutrients and antioxidants to help minimise this damage. Free radicals are unstable molecules produced by cigarette smoking, pollution and during normal metabolism. The molecules lack an electron and so "rob" other molecules to redress the balance. The term oxidation describes the process of losing an electron. Oxidation occurs thousands of times a day and inevitably causes some damage to DNA (Deoxyribonucleic acid – the genetic material of most living organisms). Although each cell can make repairs, the damage builds up and it is then that disease may develop. Therefore by eating plenty of fruit and vegetables this helps to "mop up" any damage caused.

There are various nutrients that are important in sperm production. Adequate intake of zinc,[4] the antioxidant vitamins A, C and E and selenium are essential for sperm count, shape and motility[5].

Important nutrients for men
- Zinc – found in high concentrations in sperm. Food sources include nuts, whole grains, pulses and tofu.

- Vitamin A (retinol and beta-carotene) – pre-formed Vitamin A is found naturally only in animal foods and vegans obtain this vitamin from beta-carotene, which is converted in the body to vitamin A. It is an important antioxidant which protects against tissue damage. Food sources of beta-carotene include carrots, green leafy vegetables, dried apricots and fortified margarine.

- Vitamin B12 – all vegans need to ensure a regular intake of fortified foods or a supplement. The Department of Health recommends 1.5mcg/day but as there are variations in absorption and there is no known toxicity, research suggests that higher levels may be beneficial. Studies suggest a daily intake of 3mcg from fortified foods in two or more meals or 10mcg (or 2000mcg once a week) from a supplement may be prudent.

- Vitamin C (ascorbic acid) – an antioxidant that reduces the tendency of sperm to stick together, thus making it easier for them to swim singly towards their target. Abundant in the vegan diet, found in vegetables and fruits. The UK dietary recommendations are for a minimum of five portions of fruits and vegetables per day but the US National Cancer Institute has recently increased the advice to nine per day for men and seven per day for women[6].

- Vitamin E – an antioxidant that improves sperm function, especially when the sperm binds to the egg. Plentiful in the vegan diet, found in whole grains, nuts, seeds and vegetable oils.

- Selenium – may enhance male fertility[5]. A deficiency of this mineral can affect sperms' ability to swim correctly (motility). Much better to get this nutrient from foods but if you decide to take a supplement, choose a multi-vitamin and mineral supplement containing 75mcg of selenium per day. Food sources include nuts, seeds, wholegrains, bananas and soya beans but the amount of selenium found in these foods are highly variable due to variable soil concentrations.

Keeping well

If you take alcohol, exclude it from your diet or aim for less than three to four units per day (one unit is equivalent to approximately one measure of spirit (25ml), half a pint of beer, one small (125ml) glass of wine. Regular heavy drinking (more than four units per day) can reduce the number of sperm produced and possibly damage them. If you smoke, give up. Smoking can actually reduce fertility by lowering sex hormones thus reducing the quantity of sperm produced and can also lower the quality of sperm[7]. Recent research has shown that children born to fathers who smoke are at greater risk of childhood cancers and cot death. It appears that the sperm of a man who smokes equivalent to or more than 20 cigarettes a day is only half as likely as a non-smoker to penetrate and fertilise his partner's egg. Pregnancies conceived by men who smoke are more likely to miscarry.

It has been suggested that soya, which contains phytoestrogens, may detrimentally affect sperm production or other reproductive functions. The evidence does not support this suggestion and soya foods as part of a healthy eating diet are encouraged[8].

If you are overweight, try to correct it. If you like cakes, biscuits and sweets try replacing these with small portions of homemade cakes made with wholemeal flour and less sugar or add fresh fruit. Replace sugary drinks with fruit juices and water. Studies have suggested environmental exposures and pesticides can lodge in fat stores[1]. In addition, if men are overweight, this may affect production of oestrogen which may reduce the sperm count. As mentioned, sperm counts are falling and one of the reasons may be because men are getting fatter!

Regular exercise is also very important.

FEMALE NUTRITION

Eating a healthy diet before you are pregnant will benefit your baby by giving your body a store of nutrients for the baby to draw on during pregnancy. Few studies have looked at women's nutritional status prior to and during early pregnancy but evidence suggests that this is a vulnerable period[1]. Ideally, try to follow a healthy diet for at least six months prior to conception. Nutritional health is cumulative and how well your body can nourish your baby depends not only on what you eat during your pregnancy but on how well you have been eating for years. Therefore, it is very important that lifestyle changes are made prior to pregnancy.

Keeping well

It has been suggested that pollutants such as pesticides, herbicides and exhaust fumes, accumulate in the fatty tissues of the mother and are passed onto the next generation across the placenta[9,10,11]. Fat stores are mobilised during pregnancy and may disrupt the development of the baby's hormonal systems. By eating a diet rich in fruit and vegetables which contain antioxidants, these antioxidants can help to 'mop up' the pollutants that attack the body day to day. If you smoke, give up. Numerous studies have proved the damage to the unborn child[12]. Alcohol is best avoided if you are trying to conceive. The Department of Health advises that to minimise the risk to the unborn child, women who are pregnant or trying to conceive should not drink more than one to two units of alcohol once or twice a week and should avoid binge drinking ie more than three units per day. (see page 10 for explanation of units)

Important nutrients for women

There are only two supplements that are needed during this time; vitamin B12 and folic acid. You need to ensure a reliable source of vitamin B12. Either a daily intake of 3mcg from food or 10mcg from tablets or 2000mcg tablet once a week.

Folic acid is a B vitamin and a supplement is recommended for all women, vegan, and non-vegan, wishing to conceive. A supplement of 400mcg (0.4mg) per day is recommended from the time you start trying to have a baby to the 12th week of pregnancy. In recent years folic acid supplementation has been shown to prevent neural tube defects (NTDs)[13,14,15,16]. These can occur during the first month after conception when babies' spines are developing. Taking a folic acid supplement helps reduce the risk of your baby having a neural tube defect - an abnormality caused by the brain and spinal cord failing to develop properly - such as spina bifida. If you are already pregnant, start taking a supplement immediately and continue doing so until the end of your 12th week of pregnancy. Do not worry if you are more than 12 weeks pregnant and have not taken folic acid. Taking folic acid is just a precautionary measure to reduce the risk of neural tube defects – not taking it does not necessarily mean that your baby will have a neural tube defect. Most babies are born perfectly healthy. Vegan diets are generally high in folic acid - found in green leafy vegetables, nuts, beans, yeast extracts and some fortified foods but as a safeguard, a folic acid supplement is encouraged. You must also ensure an adequate source of iodine (see pages 59-60).

Chapter 1

Key vegan nutrients for making a healthy baby

Nutrient	Sources	Requirement
Protein	Wholegrains, nuts, seeds, soya products and pulses	To provide the building blocks for new tissue
Carbohydrate	Wholegrains, pulses, fruit and potatoes	The main source of energy for your body
Essential fatty acids	Soya, walnuts, linseed	Important for the brain and nervous system
Vitamins		
● Beta-carotene (pro-vitamin A)	Carrots, green leafy vegetables, dried apricots, mango	For growth and development of tissues
● Folic acid (supplement recommended 400mcg per day)	Green leafy vegetables, yeast extracts, pulses, nuts	To prevent spina bifida and other neural tube defects of the newborn
● Riboflavin Vitamin B2	Wholegrains, yeast extracts, pulses, nuts, mushrooms, avocados	For energy metabolism
● Vitamin B12 (supplement may be needed – 3mcg /day from food or 10mcg /day from supplement)	Fortified soya products, some yeast extracts, fortified non-dairy milks and fortified cereals	Builds genetic material, DNA, and important for cell reproduction
● Vitamin C	Citrus fruits, green vegetables, potatoes, berry fruits	Helps absorb iron and resist infection
● Vitamin D	Action of sunlight on skin, margarines, fortified non-dairy milks	Keeps blood calcium at optimal levels and supports bone health
Minerals		
● Calcium	Nuts, seeds, pulses, figs, grains, fortified non-dairy milks	Important for bone health
● Iron	Nuts, seeds, pulses, dried fruit, sea vegetables, green leafy vegetables	Important for oxygen transport, immune system functioning and cellular energy
● Zinc	Wholegrains, nuts, pulses, tofu and some vegetables and fortified breakfast cereals	Important for immunity, growth and metabolism
● Iodine	Sea vegetables, Vecon yeast extract, kelp tablets	An essential component of hormones produced by the thyroid gland and required for brain development

Try to include a variety of foods every day - see the plate model on pages 4-5 for detailed information on ensuring a balanced diet. When considering supplements, check with your health care provider or contact the Vegan Society for a suitable combination.

Finally, exercise. If you are fit, you will be able to cope better with the inevitable weight gain and tiredness of pregnancy. However, if you are not used to regular exercise, start very slowly with something gentle eg swimming or walking. Regular exercise eg 3 times per week is better for you than one session of vigorous exercise.

Summary

- Try to follow a healthy diet for at least six months prior to conception

- Ensure a reliable source of at least 3mcg per day of vitamin B12

- Women are recommended to supplement their diet with 400mcg folic acid per day

- Add crumbled seaweed or Vecon to dishes to ensure an adequate iodine intake

- Do not smoke and avoid passive smoking

- Reduce or cut out alcohol

- Normalise weight

- Avoid over the counter medicines and supplements unless you have checked with your health worker

- Keep active

- Feel good about yourself and all you are doing to get yourself into tip-top pre-conceptual health!

Chapter 2

References for Chapter 2

1 Chapin RE Robbins WA Schieve LA Sweeney AM Tabacova SA Tomashek KM (2004) *Off to a good start: the influence of pre- and periconceptional exposures parental fertility and nutrition on children's health* Environmental Health Perspectives 112 1 69-78

2 Giwercman A & Bonde JP (1998) *Declining male fertility and environmental factors* Endocrinology & Metabolism Clinics of North America 27 807-830

3 Calloway DH (1983) *Nutrition and reproductive function of men* Nutrition Abstracts & Reviews 53 361-377

4 Bedwal RS Bahuguna A (1994) *Zinc copper and selenium in reproduction* Experientia Jul 15 50 (7) 626-40

5 Brown KM Arthur JR (2001) *Selenium selenoproteins and human health: a review* Publish Health Nutr Apr 4 (2B) 593-9 Review

6 Gottlieb S (2003) *Men should eat nine servings of fruit and vegetables a day* BMJ Vol 326 7397 1003 15 March 2003

7 Kulikauskas V Blaustein D Ablin RJ (1985) *Cigarette smoking and its possible effects on sperm* Fertil Steril Oct 44(4) 526-8

8 COT (2003) (Committee on toxicity of Chemicals in Food, Consumer Products & the Environment) *Phytoestrogens and health* The Food Standards Agency London

9 Chapin RE Robbins WA Schieve LA Sweeney AM Tabacova SA Tomashek KM (2004) *Off to a good start: the influence of pre- and periconceptional exposures parental fertility and nutrition on children's health* Environmental Health Perspectives 112 (1) 69-78

10 Jacobson JL Jacobson SW (1996) *Intellectual impairment in children exposed to polychlorinated biphenyls in intero* N Engl J Med 335 783-789

11 Evans HJ Fletcher J Torrance M Hargreave TB (1981) *Sperm abnormalities and cigarette smoking* Lancet Mar 21 1 (8221) 627-9

12 Ashmead GG (2003) *Smoking and pregnancy* J Matern Fetal Neonatal Med Nov 14(5) 297-304

13 Lumley J Watson L Bower C (2001) *Periconceptional supplementation with folate and/or multivitamins for preventing neural tube defects (Cochrane Review)* In: The Cochrane Library Issue 2 Oxford UK Update Software

14 Czeizel AE Dudas I (1992) *Prevention of the first occurrence of neural tube defects by periconceptional vitamin supplementation* New England Journal of Medicine 327 1832-1835

15 Smithells RW Sheppard S (1980) *Possible prevention of neural tube defects by periconceptional vitamin supplementation* Lancet ii 339-340

16 Medical Research Council Vitamin Study Group (MRCVS) (1991) *Prevention of neural tube defects: results of the MRC Vitamin Study* Lancet 238 131-137

Pregnancy

There is no doubt that a vegan diet can support healthy pregnancies and reduce the risk of many of the food borne illnesses that pose a particular threat to pregnant women. In addition, cow's milk, eggs and cheese contain saturated fat and cholesterol and are not needed for a healthy diet. A large study in the USA[1] looked at the diet of vegan women and found that they had healthy pregnancies and only one of these women (0.1%) suffered with pre-eclampsia (a syndrome of high blood pressure, reduced blood flow to the placenta and premature delivery) compared with 5-10% for the general population. Nevertheless, during this time you will be besieged by well meaning non-vegan friends, family and health professionals questioning whether a vegan diet can support pregnancy. Yes it can!

REASSURING THE PROFESSIONALS

If you are already vegan then maybe you have run the gauntlet with family and friends, eaten well, stayed healthy and people have accepted that you are not going through a fad and that you know what you are doing. But now you are pregnant. Suddenly, you may be questioned by family, friends and health professionals as to whether you are going to stay vegan and whether you are going to 'make' the baby be vegan too.

It can come as a shock to have to defend your life choices and principles to friends and strangers alike. Often when pregnant, you feel tired and emotional. Clumsy questions from people who probably haven't a clue about their own nutritional intake can be infuriating and upsetting. Hopefully, this book will help to give you the confidence you need to face these possible situations.

Health visitors do good work and can offer much needed support. However, just like other health workers they may be suspicious of anyone living an 'alternative' lifestyle. You may find their response to your veganism to be a sharp intake of breath and quick fire questions such as "What about calcium and protein?". It is their business to ensure you are eating correctly so, if you can, try and reassure them, or at least be prepared to assert that you know what you are doing. If you can demonstrate that you are 'in control' you are likely to be left alone. You may be asked to give additional blood tests. Try and view this positively. If you are eating properly, your blood results will be good and then there is no more argument! If you feel you are being pressurized by your health professional and you are feeling anxious about your appointments, then take someone else along with you for moral support.

NUTRITIONAL REQUIREMENTS DURING PREGNANCY

Eating a well balanced vegan diet during pregnancy will get your baby off to an excellent start. A nutritious diet is important to ensure correct formation of organs such as the brain, nervous system and heart. What you eat also influences the size of the placenta – the organ which acts as a lifeline between mother and child - and the composition of your blood supply which will supply oxygen and nourishment to the baby.

Pregnancy normally lasts 37-42 weeks, with the average pregnancy being 40 weeks. It is split into three trimesters, each trimester being three months. Your health visitor should provide you with a book explaining the stages of pregnancy and childbirth.

During this time of rapid growth there is an increased demand for many nutrients but the increase in energy requirements is relatively small. This is because your body becomes more efficient and makes better use of the energy you obtain from the food you eat – so you don't need to eat for two! (The three main food groups that provide energy, or calories, are carbohydrates, fats and protein). The energy requirements increase by approximately 200-300 kcals (calories) per day in the second and third trimesters, to cover the extra work of forming the baby, maintaining the placenta and carrying the extra weight. Special consideration should be given to these increased requirements but a well balanced vegan diet will easily meet these extra needs. The extra energy requirement is approximately equivalent to a bowl of cereal and non-dairy milk OR one small tin of beans on toast OR a large banana and large glass of fruit juice OR a jacket potato and margarine. Adding nutritious snacks to your daily routine is one way to get extra calories.

It should be remembered that the vegan diet possibly has the edge on omnivorous diets, more closely meeting the Department of Health recommendations [2] – low in saturated fat, high in starchy carbohydrates, dietary fibre, fruit and vegetables. Nevertheless, it doesn't hurt to give your body and your growing baby an extra boost by making sure your diet is even healthier than normal by making sure you include a wide variety of foods (see 'Balance of Good Health' on pages 4-5)

Menu idea for pregnancy

The following sample menu provides approximately 2300 kcals, 60g protein and the daily recommended amounts of calcium, iron, zinc and folate.

**** Breakfast ****
Bowl of muesli or porridge and fruit
Fortified non-dairy milk or soya yoghurt
1 slice of wholemeal/granary bread
Margarine/nut butter
Small glass of fruit juice

**** Morning snack ****
Fresh fruit
Glass of water/fruit juice

**** Lunch ****
Lentil soup
1 slice of wholemeal/granary bread
Fresh fruit

**** Mid-afternoon snack ****
Home-made fruit cake
Glass of water/fruit juice

**** Tea ****
TVP Shepherds pie and steamed vegetables
Fruit crumble and ice cream
eg Swedish Glace, Tofutti Rock & Roll

**** Supper ****
Wholegrain crackers and tahini
Glass of fortified non-dairy milk or soya yoghurt
(+ vit B12 fortified foods or supplement)

IMPORTANT NUTRIENTS DURING PREGNANCY

The Department of Health recommended nutrient intakes (RNIs) are based on omnivores and it has to be questioned whether vegans have the same requirements because they may store nutrients more efficiently [3].

Folic acid/folate

Folic acid is a B vitamin of crucial importance in early pregnancy to help protect against neural tube defects such as spina bifida[4]. Vegan diets are usually rich in this B vitamin and studies have shown vegan women typically have higher intakes than omnivores. It has to be questioned, therefore, whether a folic acid supplement is necessary. Although a supplement is unlikely to be required for vegans, because toxicity from high intakes is rare, it is prudent that all women planning a pregnancy take a supplement of 400mcg and continue up to the 12th week of pregnancy. Folic acid is not stored in the body so daily intakes of foods supplying this vitamin are important (see table on page 18). Folic acid dissolves in water and cooking food for too long will destroy it. The shorter the cooking time, and the less water you use, the better. Stir frying is a quick and effective way to cook food without losing too much folic acid.

Vitamin A (beta-carotene)

Vitamin A is found naturally only in animal foods and vegans obtain this vitamin from beta-carotene in plant foods and other pro-vitamin A carotenoids which is converted in the body to vitamin A. By law in Britain, vitamin A (as retinol or beta-carotene) is added to margarine, which is a major source for the general population. This vitamin is important for growth and maintenance of the foetus. Although small amounts of vitamin A are essential for health, too much can cause deformities in the developing baby and pregnant women are advised to avoid excessive intakes in the form of supplements or as liver products – not a concern for vegans! Accordingly vitamin A supplements should be avoided. Sources of carotene from which vitamin A is made are safe. Sources include orange fruits and vegetables, broccoli, green leafy vegetables and prunes.

Vitamin B12

This can be stored in our bodies but it cannot be stressed enough how important it is to ensure a reliable source of vitamin B12. Vitamin B12 needs are no higher during pregnancy as it is assumed that body stores are sufficient. The Department of Health recommend 1.5mcg/day. However, as there is no known toxicity, a higher daily intake of 3mcg from fortified foods in two or more meals or a 10mcg supplement may be prudent to ensure that your baby is born with adequate stores. This vitamin is essential for the formation of red blood cells and a healthy nervous system and adequate B12 enhances the uptake of folate from our food. It is also produced by micro organisms in the small intestines of humans and animals but it is not well absorbed and retained in humans. Therefore a regular intake is recommended.

Vitamin B12 is not produced by plants but is synthesised by bacteria, yeasts, moulds and some algae. Some plant foods can contain vitamin B12 on their surface from soil residues but this is not a reliable source of vitamin B12. It has been reported that B12 exists in some non-animal foods such as spirulina, sea vegetables, tempeh and miso. While spirulina and sea vegetables can contain the active form of vitamin B12, they are also known to contain inactive B12 or B12 analogues. This form of vitamin B12 cannot perform the functions of true B12. Some of the active B12 is converted to B12 analogues during the drying process. For this reason these products are not considered reliable B12 sources. Fermented foods such as tempeh and miso were found to contain variable amounts of B12 when they were manufactured in unsanitary conditions. Today they are generally fermented in clean stainless steel vats and contain little, if any, vitamin B12 For reliable sources of vitamin B12, choose fortified foods such as certain non-dairy milks, yeast extracts and breakfast cereals.

Important nutrients during pregnancy

Nutrient	Uses and requirements
Folic Acid/Folate (B vitamin)	To form the baby's new tissue and blood supply A supplement of 400mcg/day up to 12th week of pregnancy. Women with diabetes have an increased requirement (see your health advisor) 5mg/day in women with a family history of neural tube defect and women who have epilepsy
Vitamin B12	Ensure adequate intake to provide baby with sufficient stores at birth and to provide enough for breastfeeding 3mcg/day from fortified food or 10mcg/day from a supplement[#]
Riboflavin (Vitamin B2)	Increased by 0.3mg/day to 1.4mg/day* to meet the needs of the growing foetus and for the riboflavin content of breast milk
Vitamin C	To help baby's tissue formation. Increased by 10mg during the 3rd trimester, to 50mg* day.
Vitamin D	Essential for the increased calcium absorption. Requirement of 10mcg* per day
Vitamin A (beta-carotene)	For growth and maintenance of the foetus. Requirement of an extra 100mcg per day, raising the maternal requirement to 700mcg per day
Calcium	Calcium absorption increases in pregnancy and may compensate for increased needs. 700 mg/day*
Iron	Iron is needed for increased maternal blood volume and to form the baby's blood. 14.8mg/day*
Zinc	Requirements increase during pregnancy but easily met through diet and no increment required. Zinc is needed for growth and development of the foetus. 7.0mg/day*
Iodine	An essential component of hormones produced by the thyroid gland. No increase during pregnancy. 140mcg/day
Protein	Requirements increase during pregnancy by 10g/day to 51g for the maintenance of new tissue

*Based on RNI (Department of Health recommended nutrient intake 1991)

[#]This is higher than the Department of Health recommendation of 1.5mcg/day.

Sources
Green leafy vegetables, fortified breakfast cereals, nuts, yeast extract, oranges, beans, peanuts, wheatgerm, brussel sprouts, green beans.
Fortified foods eg some non-dairy milks, TVP, yeast extracts and cereals; B12 tablets
Fortified cereals, pulses, vegetables, wholegrains
Found in fruit and vegetables - plentiful in the vegan diet
Exposure to sunlight is main source of this vitamin. Fortified cereals, margarine and some non-dairy milks
Easily met by the vegan diet from orange fruit and vegetables, broccoli, green leafy vegetables and prunes
Green leafy vegetables, tahini, almonds, figs, fortified non-dairy milks, fortified cereals, tofu (processed with calcium sulphate), tap water in hard water areas and some bottled waters
Fortified cereals, pulses, dried fruit and green vegetables. Eating citrus fruits with iron rich foods can increase iron absorption.
Peas, beans, brown rice, spinach, nuts, tofu and tempeh
Seaweed, kelp tablets, Vecon
Beans, nuts, seeds, pulses

If you are not taking foods fortified with vitamin B12, ensure you take a supplement. When reading labels look for 'cyanocobalamin' or 'cobalamin' – these are the most absorbable forms of vitamin B12. All B12 includes a cobalamin core, cyanocobalamin is the most stable form and is therefore favoured for fortification. The cobalamin compounds used for supplements and fortified foods are more reliably absorbed than cobalamin from meat.

The B12 stores of infants at birth are dependent upon the levels of this vitamin circulating in the maternal blood stream during pregnancy – the foetus scavenges B12 from the mother and healthy newborns are found to have twice their mothers' levels of B12! It is also particularly important that your B12 stores are sufficient so that breast milk levels of B12 meet baby's needs. Although the body has the ability to store and recycle this vitamin in the liver, mums-to-be should not rely on stores as there is some uncertainty as to the impact of vitamin B12 stores on the vitamin B12 status of the baby. Some studies suggest that stores are not available to the infant and that the baby's vitamin B12 status relies on nutritional intake[5].

Riboflavin (vitamin B2)
The growing foetus demands an extra 0.3mg per day which is easily met by the vegan diet. Extra riboflavin is also required for the production of breast milk. Sources include fortified cereals, wheatgerm, pulses, almonds, mushrooms and yeast extract.

Vitamin C
Extra vitamin C is needed during pregnancy to help the baby's tissue formation but this can easily be met by consuming lots of fruit and vegetables but remember once you peel or cut fruit and vegetables and they are exposed to air, you start to lose vitamin C, and it is also lost in cooking. So keep fruit and vegetables as whole as possible and cook quickly in minimal water. Potatoes are a good source of vitamin C and provide extra vitamins and fibre if cooked and eaten with their skins.

Try to include some source of vitamin C at each meal. A daily intake of vitamin C is essential because the body does not store this vitamin. Vitamin C helps the body absorb iron, important for the extra demand of the developing baby and maternal blood volume.

Vitamin D

Requirements for vitamin D are increasing during this time because of the need for extra calcium to form the baby's bones and to produce milk. Vitamin D is necessary for the absorption of calcium. Vitamin D is found naturally only in animal foods as vitamin D3 (cholecalciferol) but most people get sufficient vitamin D via the action of sunlight on the skin but whether the increased needs during pregnancy can be met in this way is not clear. Therefore, the Department of Health recommends if sun exposure is limited, a vitamin D supplement may be necessary[6]. Again, vegans generally tend to be more health conscious than their omnivore peers and ensure they get plenty of fresh air and exposure to sunlight. If you are concerned, check with your health care provider before taking supplements and if taken, aim to achieve an intake of 10mcg/day. Vegan food sources of this vitamin rely on fortified foods such as margarine, fortified cereals, and some fortified non-dairy milks. The vegan source of vitamin D is vitamin D2 (ergocalciferol) which is made from fungal or plant sources. D3 is made from fish oil or lanolin. Be aware that most fortified cereals in supermarkets just state vitamin D on the ingredients list without specifying whether this is vitamin D2 (from vegetable source) or vitamin D3 (from animal source) and on investigation more often than not it is from the cheaper and more easily available animal source of D3. The D2 source is invariably shown on cereals in health food stores.

Calcium

Studies have shown that the calcium intake of vegans may be below current recommendations and this frequently raises concerns, particularly as calcium needs are high in pregnancy. However evidence suggests that although vegans consume less calcium in their foods, they use it and store it more efficiently than omnivores. In addition, it should be remembered that the body has the ability to compensate if intake is low and during pregnancy the efficiency of calcium absorption rises. No adverse effects of vegan diets during pregnancy have been reported. Nevertheless, it is sensible to ensure a good calcium intake.

The main source of calcium for omnivores is dairy produce. When you stop to consider that humans drink the milk of another species, this practice is unnatural. Dairy sources are also linked to saturated fat and cholesterol. Non-dairy calcium sources include green leafy vegetables, almonds, figs, seeds and fortified non dairy milks which are not associated with cholesterol and saturated fat.

Iron

There is an extra demand for iron for the developing baby and to form haemoglobin, which is the oxygen carrier in the blood. Sufficient iron is essential for the increased maternal blood volume and for the formation of the baby's blood. However, due to cessation of periods and increased intestinal absorption, no extra iron intake is required.

Although vegan diets are higher in total iron content than omnivorous diets, studies have shown that iron stores are lower in vegans because the iron from plant foods, non haem iron, is not so well absorbed[7]. However iron deficiency anaemia rates are no different in vegans than omnivores. The higher vitamin C content of vegan diets improves iron absorption. Therefore if you add a glass of fruit juice or piece of fruit to a meal, your body will take in around twice as much iron. Anaemia can be a problem during any pregnancy, regardless of your diet, so all pregnant women need to eat foods rich in iron. The tannin in tea can reduce your absorption of iron so if drinking tea, try to have this between rather than with meals.

Check with your health advisor if you believe your iron stores are low. High doses of iron supplements can interfere with zinc and copper absorption and so should be avoided if possible. They can also lead to constipation, a common problem in pregnancy.

Zinc

The requirement for zinc during pregnancy is believed to increase but this has not been proven and no benefits from supplements have been shown. It is likely that a pregnant woman adapts to ensure an adequate intake of zinc for the growing baby. Ensure a mixture of zinc rich foods such as nuts*, seeds, beans and cereals. Sprouting zinc rich beans and seeds are a useful insurance policy.

WEIGHT GAIN

The pattern of weight gain is different for each woman but a general trend is to have little weight gain for the first 12 weeks. Then in the second and third trimesters a weight gain of half a kilogram (1lb) a week is common. Energy requirements increase by approximately 200-300 kcals per day in the second and third trimesters to allow for the mother's body to change and the baby to grow.

An optimal weight gain of 12.5kg (28lb) is the figure used for an average pregnancy. Average weight gains are between 11 and 16kg but the variability is very large and depends on your weight before pregnancy.

If there is little weight increase or if it is slow, try to eat more food. Eating little and often and ensuring your diet includes energy dense foods

that are lower in bulk may help eg dried fruit, tahini, margarine, oils, nuts* and seeds. If your weight gain seems too quick, you may be eating too many refined, sugary or fatty foods. Try to replace these with higher fibre, low fat options such as fruits, vegetables, grains and legumes. Complications caused by excessive gains in weight are similar to those due to overweight and obesity. However, this is not the time to diet and deplete your body of nutrients.

FLUID

It is suggested that the average sedentary pregnant women should drink a minimum of 2 litres of fluid daily, preferably water, to increase body fluid and reduce problems with constipation. Fruit and vegetables contribute to your water intake providing around 90% water in a form that is very easy for the body to use.

Alcohol

Alcohol is not recommended for any pregnant women or a woman contemplating pregnancy. In addition, animal derived ingredients are used in many beers and wines, making them unsuitable. Alcohol passes through the placenta and has been shown to reduce placental uptake and transport of nutrients, decreasing foetal blood glucose, reducing blood flow to the placenta, and interfering with protein synthesis in foetal tissues. This puts the unborn child at risk of birth defects. The Department of Health advises that to minimise the risk to the unborn child, women who are pregnant or trying to conceive should not drink more than one to two units of alcohol once or twice a week and should avoid binge drinking ie more than three units per day.

However, a recent report by the Royal College of Obstetricians and Gynaecologists suggests that alcohol consumption in excess of three units a week during the first trimester increases the risk of miscarriage[8].

* It may be prudent to avoid nuts if there is a history of allergy

One unit of alcohol is equivalent to half a pint of ordinary beer OR a single measure of a spirit OR a small glass of sherry OR a small glass of wine. In order to avoid any risk, it is advisable to stay away from alcohol consumption during pregnancy.

Caffeine

Many people who are concerned about their health choose to avoid caffeine. It is eliminated from a woman's body slowly and crosses the placenta to the foetus[9]. There have been concerns that it might lead to birth defects or miscarriages. The Food Standards Agency advises that pregnant woman should moderate their caffeine intake to no more than 300mg/day[10] which is equivalent to approximately four cups of coffee per day. Unfortunately it is virtually impossible to give precise guidelines in terms of cups of coffee per day because there is such great variation in the caffeine content of a cup of coffee and coffee is not the only source of caffeine in the diet eg tea, cola and chocolate also contain caffeine. However, the following table is provided as a guide to the caffeine content of drinks and chocolate so you can get an idea of your daily intake.

Consumer guidance on caffeine intake

	Caffeine content
Cup or mug of tea	1-90mg
Cup or mug of instant coffee	21-120mg
Cup or mug of brewed coffee	15-254mg
Can of cola	30mg
Can of stimulant drink	80mg
Serving of coffee/chocolate dessert	30mg
Bar of chocolate	15mg

Note: Actual content may vary considerably from these figures.
Ref: Thomas B (2003) Caffeine and Health: A Review Unilever Best Foods and Food Standards Agency

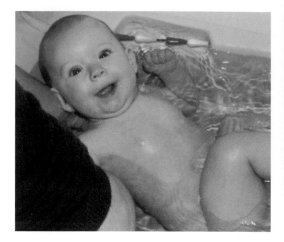

COMMON NUTRITIONAL PROBLEMS DURING PREGNANCY

Anaemia

Worldwide, iron deficiency is the most common nutritional deficiency but studies show that the iron status of pregnant vegan women is usually normal and iron deficiency is no more common than in the general population. The midwife will probably take blood three times during pregnancy, around weeks 10, 16 and 36 which will included checking your blood group and iron status (see table on page 59 for iron rich foods). However, if there is a risk of iron deficiency it is wise to only drink tea between meals and to wait at least one hour after eating before drinking tea as the tannin in tea limits the absorption of iron from plant foods.

Constipation and haemorrhoids (piles)

Constipation is a common problem during pregnancy and whether it is less common in vegans who consume a high fibre diet is unknown. Constipation occurs because of hormonal changes associated with pregnancy and can be worsened by iron supplements. If it is a problem for you, be sure to drink plenty of liquid, eat lots of wholegrains and take gentle daily exercise eg walking.

If you are also suffering with piles, a high fibre diet, gentle exercise and plenty of liquid may also help.

Morning sickness

Nausea and vomiting, especially in early pregnancy, affects about seven in ten women but in only the minority of cases is the condition severe enough for medical intervention. The causes of nausea, vomiting and food aversions in pregnancy are not fully understood. Changes in hormone levels, gut motility and heightened senses of taste and smell have all been suggested.

Although there is no absolute cure for pregnancy sickness, some of the following tips may help:

- Try to eat something every few hours because morning sickness can be worse when you haven't eaten for a while. Nausea can be caused by hunger. Try eating small frequent meals based on starchy carbohydrates such as bread, bananas and cereals

- Avoid greasy or fried foods as these take longer to digest

- Foods containing ginger have been found to relieve nausea for some women[11]

- When nauseous, slowly sipping a fizzy drink such as carbonated water may help

- If the smell of cooking makes you queasy, ask someone else to cook while you are out of the house or try eating cold foods like sandwiches, cereal, crackers and fruit. Snacks can be as nourishing as cooked meals

- Keep rooms well ventilated and odour free and get out in the fresh air as much as possible

- Get out of bed slowly and avoid getting up quickly after meals. Making sudden movements can worsen the nausea

- Sit for at least 15 minutes after eating

- Keep a snack like crackers or dry cereal by your bed and eat a little if you wake up in the night or before you get up in the morning

Don't worry that the constant sickness will affect your baby. Women who have morning sickness have babies who are just as healthy as women who don't suffer from morning sickness. However, if the sickness continues, discuss this with your health advisor.

Heartburn and indigestion

This can occur at any time during pregnancy but is more common later in the pregnancy when the baby displaces or squashes the internal organs. Individual women usually learn which foods to avoid and choose to prevent or alleviate these conditions.

- Try to eat small frequent meals

- Do not rush meals

- Drink liquids between rather than with meals

- Avoid spicy foods and fizzy drinks

- Stay upright after eating and if eating in the evening, leave at least two hours before going to bed

- If it is a problem at night, a slightly tilted bed or pillows to prop up can help

FOODS TO BE AVOIDED

There has been concern about the safety of certain foods during pregnancy. There are some foods which are potentially harmful to an unborn baby. These foods may contain bacteria such as listeria and salmonella, or they may have high levels of vitamin A – these are all animal foods!

The majority of cases of food poisoning are due to meat and dairy products. The only foods that vegans need to be careful with are vegetables and salads, which should be washed carefully as any soil they have been in contact with may be contaminated and cause toxoplasmosis. Toxoplasmosis is caused by an organism called Toxoplasma gondii and has been found in cat faeces. Make sure all food is stored, cooked correctly and eaten within the recommended date.

Some commonsense points:

● Always wash hands before and after preparing food

● Wash all fruits, vegetables and salad

● Cool left over food quickly and consume within 24 hours

● Make sure your fridge/freezer is running at correct temperature

● Do not re-heat rice

● Do not re-freeze foods

● Take extra care to wash your hands thoroughly if changing cat litter trays

Soya

Recently there have been a number of unfounded scares over the safety of soya for pregnant or breastfeeding women. Some reports have suggested that the oestrogenic effects of the soya plant could affect the sexual development of boys born to vegetarian mothers[12] but these results have not been shown to be statistically significant and the UK Committee on Toxicity of Chemicals in Food concluded that there were "no adverse clinical effects on sexual development or reproductive health" and that soya can safely be included as part of a healthy diet[13].

Artificial sweeteners

These are classified as food additives and their use is controlled by The Sweeteners in Foods Regulations 1995. They are based on acceptable daily intakes (ADIs) that can be taken over a lifetime without known health risk to anyone, including pregnant women. They can cross the placenta and are eliminated very slowly from foetal tissues but have not been shown to be harmful to the developing baby. However as a precautionary measure, they are best left out of the diet. Sweeten food with natural sweeteners such as fruit and fruit juice. If you need to, use a small amount of sugar or preferably molasses.

Peanuts

If you suffer from diagnosed allergic conditions or where the father or any other children in the family has a history of allergy eg eczema, asthma, hayfever, urticaria (itchy skin and rashes), rhinitis (recurrent sneezing and watering of the nose) or food allergy, you may wish to avoid eating peanuts for the period of time that you are pregnant. This is because the development of allergy is known to have genetic links and consideration should be given to the possibility that sensitisation may occur in the womb. This is just precautionary because there has not been any conclusive evidence. Any child that is born to a family with a history of allergies is encouraged to be breastfed, preferably exclusively for six months, as exclusive breastfeeding may offer protection against the development of allergies. (see pages 47-48 covering allergies)

Summary

- Continue with folic acid up to the 12th week of pregnancy

- Include a regular source of iodine two to three times a week

- Ensure a regular reliable source of vitamin B12

- Ensure an adequate fluid intake

- Avoid alcohol

- Moderate your caffeine intake

References for Chapter 3

1 Carter JP et al (1987) *Pre-eclampsia and reproductive performance in a community of vegans* South Med J 80(6) 692-697

2 Thomas B (2003) *Caffeine and Health: A Review* Unilever Best Foods

3 Linkswiler HM Zemel MB Hegsted M Schouette S (1981) *Protein induced hypercalciuria* Fed Proc 40 2429-2433

4 Czeizel AE Dudas I (1992) *Prevention of the first occurrence of neural tube defects by periconceptional vitamin supplementation* New England Journal of Medicine 1992 327 1832-1835

Medical Research Council Vitamin Study Group (MRCVS) (1991) *Prevention of neural tube defects: results of the MRC Vitamin Study* Lancet 238 131-137

Smithells RW, Sheppard S, Schorah LJ et al (1980) *Possible prevention of neural tube defects by periconceptional vitamin supplementation* Lancet 1980 ii 339-340

5 Specker BL Black A Allen L Morrow F (1990) *Vitamin B12: low milk concentrations are related to low serum concentrations in vegetarian women and to methylmalonic aciduria in their infants* Am J Clin Nutr 52 1073-1076

6 Department of Health (1991) *Dietary reference values (DRVs) for Food Energy and Nutrients in the UK* Report on Health & Social Subjects 41 London HMSO

7 Craig WJ (1994) *Iron status of vegetarians* Am J of Clin Nutr 59 1233S-1237S

8 Royal College of Obstetricians and Gynaecologists (1999) *Alcohol Consumption in Pregnancy* London RCOG

9 Hinds IS West WL Knight EM Harland BF (1996) *The effect of caffeine on pregnancy outcome variables* Nutrition Reviews 54 203-207

10 COT (2001) (Committee on toxicity of Chemicals in Food, Consumer Products & the Environment) *Statement on the reproductive effects of caffeine* COT statement 2001/06 London: Food Standards Agency

11 Erick M (1995) *Vitamin B6 and ginger in morning sickness* JADA 95 416

12 North K Golding J (2000) *A maternal vegetarian diet in pregnancy is associated with hypospadias* Br J Urol Int 85 107-113

13 COT (2003) Committee on Toxicity of Chemicals in Food Consumer Products and the Environment. *Phytoestrogens and health* The Food Standards Agency London

Birth

If you are opting for a home birth then you will already have organized your shopping to include any easy vegan meals or snacks. If you go into hospital to have your baby then it is important to take some vegan supplies with you.

Vegan margarine and non-dairy milks are generally not provided in hospital although you may be able to get some vegan food such as jacket potatoes or cereals and toast. The more organized you can be, the more you will enjoy your short stay in hospital.

Immediately the baby is born she will be offered vitamin K. Vitamin K helps with blood clotting and the regulation of calcium in the blood. It is given routinely to newborns because infants are born with very low body stores of vitamin K and since the gut is sterile at birth, production via intestinal bacteria cannot occur initially. Although the risk is small, this low status would put 1 in 800 babies at risk of serious bleeds including intracranial bleeding (brain haemorrhage). The oral form of vitamin K contains glycocholic which is derived from the gallbladders of cows but the injection form is animal free. For the oral form, two doses are given in the first week and the third dose is given at one month of age (the third dose is omitted in formula fed babies because formula feeds contain vitamin K). Vitamin K given by a single intramuscular injection at birth is synthetic and suitable for vegans. Only these two forms of vitamin K are licenced for use in the UK. This vitamin is abundant in the vegan diet with green leafy vegetables, soya and sea vegetables being particularly rich sources.

Once your baby has been born, you will find the first eight weeks to be a rollercoaster ride of Health Visitor and GP appointments. If the baby is gaining weight and you seem ok, then you are unlikely to be badgered about your veganism – especially if you are breastfeeding for which you get a lot of gold stars! After this eight week period you are pretty much left alone. It is up to you whether you take your baby to your local Health Clinic to be weighed every fortnight or month. Seeing your baby steadily gain weight is very satisfying and reassuring, especially if this is your first baby and you need the reassurance. However, don't be anxious if another baby of the same age weighs something quite different to yours! All babies are different and vegan babies and adults tend to be lighter in weight. This is a positive thing for all sorts of health reasons. For more information and support from other vegan families, contact the Vegan Society for the Vegan Family Contacts list (see appendix).

BREASTFEEDING
Benefits of breast feeding
Up to the age of six months, the perfect food for baby is breast milk. It is difficult to replicate the complex formula of breast milk with its delicate balance of nutrients and built-in immunity which passes from mother to baby. There are substances that appear in breast milk but not in infant formulas and the importance of these is not clear. However, we do know that breast milk nourishes your baby with the complete mix of nutrients to

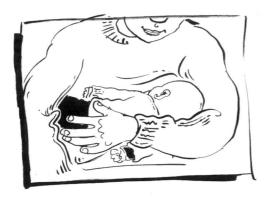

help her develop and grow and protect against certain illnesses and allergy[1]. For example, breastfeeding protects against ear infections, respiratory diseases and gastro-intestinal illness and there is a lower incidence of cot deaths in breastfed babies. Breastfed infants have been shown to produce more stable levels of lactic-acid-producing bacteria than formula fed babies. These bacteria improve intestinal microbial balance which has been proven to protect against colon disease. This protection continues throughout childhood, even after breastfeeding has stopped, with the prevention of serious health problems including diabetes[2].

Breast milk contains more cholesterol than formula feeds and studies have shown that babies who are breastfed develop into children who have better metabolic processes for the breakdown of cholesterol and therefore have lower cholesterol levels and a lower incidence of heart attack. It is now recognised that to breastfeed your baby, even for as little as two weeks, is of great value. Ideally infants should be exclusively breastfed for six months. Thereafter the WHO (World Health Organisation) recommend infants should be weaned with continued breastfeeding up to two years of age or beyond.

Most mothers produce more than enough milk to satisfy their babies and the milk produced by vegan mothers can be nutritionally as good if not better than that of non-vegan nursing mothers[3]. However, ensure a reliable and adequate source of vitamin B12 and w-3 fatty acids. Breastfed infants

of well nourished vegan mothers grow and develop normally[1] - you do not need to drink cow's milk to make milk of your own. At times you may feel concerned because you cannot actually see how much milk is being taken. The amount of milk a baby takes varies from one baby to another. Some will thrive on 600ml (about one pint) and others need 1000ml per day. Most babies take about 800-900ml a day in the first three months of life. If your baby is gaining weight satisfactorily and appears to be contented, you can be sure she is getting enough milk.

Important nutrients for the breastfed infant
Vitamin B12

It appears that only newly absorbed vitamin B12 (as opposed to the vitamin B12 that is stored in the mother's body) is passed through breast milk therefore it is essential that a dietary source of B12 or a supplement is taken by nursing mothers whilst breastfeeding[3]. A supplement of 10mcg per day or a daily source of 4mcg from foods fortified with vitamin B12 is essential, eg yeast extracts, margarines, fortified non-dairy milks and breakfast cereals.

There have been several reports of vitamin B12 deficient breastfed infants where the mother was not supplementing her diet with vitamin B12[3]. Once a supplement had been provided, recovery was quick but B12 deficiency can be fatal or result in permanent nervous system damage if not corrected in time.

Food type	mcg of Vitamin B12 per 100g/100ml
Yeast extract*	2-50mcg
Margarines*	5.0mcg
Soya milks*	0.5 - 1.6mcg
Breakfast cereals*	0.8mcg
Textured vegetable protein (TVP)*	0-25mcg
Nutritional yeast powder	0-40mcg

*fortified varieties (organic versions are NOT fortified – the Soil Association unfortunately will not accept fortification as being organic)

Fatty acids

There has been a lot of interest recently in the fatty acids important for babies' brain development[4]. Docosahexaenoic acid (DHA) is a fatty acid which appears to be important for eye and brain development in babies. It is found primarily in animal derived foods but babies can make DHA from another fatty acid called alpha-linolenic acid which is found in breast milk if the mother's diet includes good sources of this fatty acid. Good sources of alpha-linolenic acid include flaxseed oil, rapeseed (canola) oil and walnuts. Breastfeeding mothers can also supplement their diet with 1 teaspoon of flaxseed or 1 tablespoon of rapeseed oil per day which will help to achieve the right balance of fatty acids.

There are now microalgae-based DHA supplements available for those who wish to supplement the diet.

The nursing mother

Many mothers talk of the convenience of breastfeeding; the closeness and skin contact which a baby gets when feeding from its mother is comforting for the baby. Breastfeeding stimulates the release of calming and soothing hormones - wonderful for mother and baby alike! However, breastfeeding doesn't come as a second nature to all mums and in many cases it has to be learned, like any other skill. Your Health Visitor will be able to offer you a lot of helpful advice and there are organisations who can also offer help and support (see appendix).

There are lots of benefits for the breastfeeding mother too. She will benefit from a reduced risk of developing breast cancer before the menopause, the release of stress relieving hormones and it helps the uterus regain shape quickly as it contracts when baby suckles in the early days of breastfeeding. There may also be other benefits we are not aware of yet.

Nutrient requirements of the nursing mother

During breastfeeding your energy requirements will be high and they will increase as your body produces more milk to satisfy your rapidly growing baby. It is very easy to overlook your own diet and health at this time. The amount of milk produced is affected by diet. Vegan mothers have been shown to produce normal amounts of milk. Remember to eat and drink regularly; a useful tip is to have a nutritious snack and drink at your side when you are nursing, such as a banana and a glass of soya milk, bowl of cereal and fruit juice or a 'cheese' salad sandwich and glass of water.

The best diet for breastfeeding is very similar to the diet recommended for pregnancy. There is no doubt that your diet during pregnancy does affect the quality of the breast milk. Calorie, protein and vitamin B12 needs are slightly higher (see table on page 32) while the need for iron is reduced. However, there is some evidence that breastfeeding mums have a more efficient protein metabolism and so do not require extra protein. Calcium requirements increase and it is important to ensure a good calcium intake – almonds, pulses, green leafy vegetables and figs are the main sources and some fortified non-dairy milks. Drinking water also provides calcium. It is well known that adaptation to low calcium intakes does occur and also the absorption of calcium from the digestive tract is improved in pregnancy and lactation. The absorption of calcium is also aided by vitamin D which is produced by the action of sunlight on the skin and is present in margarine, fortified breakfast cereals and some non dairy milk. It is essential that the mother takes a vitamin B12 supplement (10mcg per day) or she ensures a regular source of foods fortified with vitamin B12 (4mcg per day).

Energy (calorie) requirements are increased at this time, these increase by approximately 500 calories per day. You will meet your extra requirements quite easily if you eat as you did during pregnancy and include one or two extra snacks or an additional meal a day.

If you eat too little while breastfeeding you may not produce as much milk as required. As in pregnancy, small frequent meals are the best way to be sure that you are getting enough calories and remember, a well balanced vegan diet will provide all the nutrients needed for yourself and your baby.

Make sure you drink plenty of fluid as breastfeeding is a thirsty business – breastfeeding stimulates a thirst. Expect to drink at least 1.5 litres (2.5 pints) of liquid every day. Try to choose healthy drink options such as water, fruit juice and fruit teas rather than tea, coffee and cola. Always have a drink at your side when you are feeding your baby.

Summary

- Take a vitamin B12 supplement of 10mcg per day or 4mcg from fortified food.

- Drink at least 1.5 litres (2.5 pints) of fluid per day

- Eat three meals and two good snacks a day

- Eat at least five portions of fruit and vegetables a day

- Snack on fruit, nuts and seeds rather than sugary foods

- Eat plenty of high fibre foods

Allergies

If there is a history of allergy, exclusive breastfeeding for the first six months is ideal. Studies are inconclusive about the effects of diet during breastfeeding on the development of food allergies. As a precautionary measure if you suffer from an allergic condition such as asthma and hayfever or atopic skin disorders such as eczema or where the father or a sibling of the child has a clinical history of such conditions, you may wish to avoid eating peanuts and food containing peanut products. There is no reason for nursing mothers who do not fall into this category to avoid eating peanuts.

Some foods you eat may upset the baby's tummy if you are breastfeeding. Try and be aware of this: if your baby seems agitated, draws her legs up with tummy ache or has very runny nappies, this may be as a result of something you ate. For example some babies react to TVP (textured vegetable protein) their mothers have eaten.

Try to avoid the following:

- Caffeine passes through the milk and can cause irritability and sleeplessness in your baby as well as you

- Alcohol passes through the milk and can damage the baby's health. If you do have an occasional drink, enjoy it after the last feed of the day and avoid breastfeeding for at least four hours

- Dieting whilst you are breastfeeding may compromise your health and your milk supply. If you eat healthily, you will find that your weight will revert to normal during breastfeeding

The first few days

In the first couple of days of breastfeeding your baby is not getting milk but colostrum which protects your baby from disease and helps her excrete meconium from the bowel. Meconium is a material that collects in the intestines of a foetus and forms the first stools of a new born. The meconium builds up during the time the baby is in the womb and you will notice that the bowel movement (meconium) is dark and greenish – this is perfectly normal. After two to three days the colour changes to greenish yellow and it may be a bit loose and later it becomes a more golden yellow colour. Remember that what you eat can also affect the colour of your baby's motion. Constipation is almost unheard of in the breastfed baby. Normal stools are yellow, soft and easy to pass. It is not uncommon for a baby to go several days between opening bowels and other babies may open their bowels after every feed. Both patterns are normal. Providing your baby is well and not in discomfort there is no reason to be concerned. If it does occur, it is usually due to not enough feeds, which can lead to starvation stools which are hard and green.

Initially babies may wish to suckle every two hours or so but this settles to a more regular pattern in the first few weeks of seven to eight feeds each day, lasting about 20 minutes each. However, every child is different, be flexible and do not stick to a rigid schedule such as feeding every four hours.

The volume of breast milk consumed by an infant varies. If your baby is satisfied and growing, she is receiving sufficient milk. Studies have shown an average milk output of about 650ml per day at one month and 750ml at three months. In the first week of breastfeeding antibodies are at their highest so it is worth doing it even if it is only for a few weeks if that is all that is possible.

Breastfed babies don't need anything to drink other than breast milk. Giving water or anything else could disturb the supply on demand production of breast milk in the early weeks. The more often you feed, the more breast milk you will produce.

Most babies develop some sort of feeding routine as the weeks go by. However, many babies still have an unsettled time each day, often in the evening. Your baby may be off and on the breast a lot, only settling for short periods before crying again. You'll probably find your baby grows out of this in time which is often helped by having a routine. Most older babies feed between five and eight times a day.

Combined breast and bottle feeding in the first weeks of life may reduce the supply of your own breastmilk. If you plan to breastfeed, the safest option is not to offer a bottle at all. A bottle of formula is likely to fill your baby up so a breast feed is missed and your supply is stimulated less. If you plan on stopping breastfeeding and switching to the bottle do it gradually. Substitute one breastfeed with a bottle feed, doing away with one feed every two days so the complete switch takes place over 10 to 15 days.

Expressing milk

This can be useful if you need to be away from your baby when you would normally feed her or if your baby is ill and unable to come to the breast. Your baby will let you know how much she needs but a rough guide is 2.5oz (approximately 60mls) of milk per 0.5kg (1lb) of body weight in 24 hours. Remember, expressing will stimulate your supply so it won't reduce the amount produced.

Summary

- Make sure you are well nourished to breastfeed your baby
- Ensure a daily intake of vitamin B12
- Remember to eat and drink regularly
- Avoid eating peanuts and peanut products if there is a history of allergies in the family
- Avoid caffeine and alcohol
- Ensure adequate calcium and vitamin D fortified foods

For further advice and support in breastfeeding see Appendix.

BOTTLE FEEDING

Breastfeeding is best for your baby for numerous reasons (see breastfeeding section). However, if for some reason you are unable to breastfeed there is nothing to worry about and no reason to feel guilty or inadequate. Millions of healthy babies are bottle fed.

Nutrients important for the nursing mother

Nutrient	Requirement	Sources
Protein	Additional 11g/day giving a total of 56g/day. This is easily met by the extra snacks and foods needed to provide extra calories	Beans, nuts#, seeds and pulses
Vitamin B12	Additional 0.5mcg/day. The Vegan Society recommends a total daily intake of 4mcg from fortified foods or 10mcg from a supplement*	Fortified foods eg some non dairy milks, cereals, TVP, yeast extract, B12 tablets or powder
Vitamin A (Carotenoids)	Additional 350mcg/day giving a total of 950mcg/day	Fruits, vegetables and margarine
Folic Acid/Folate (B vitamin)	Additional 60mcg/day to 260mcg/day	Green leafy vegetables, fortified breakfast cereals, peanuts, wheatgerm, brussel sprouts, green beans
Riboflavin (Vitamin B2)	An extra 0.5mg per day to 1.6mg/day	Fortified cereals, pulses, vegetables, wholegrains
Vitamin C	Additional 30mg/day to 70mg/day	Fruits and vegetables
Vitamin D	Additional 10mcg/day to 20mcg/day (may need supplement check with health care provider)	Vitamin D is synthesized in our skin with sunlight exposure. Vegan food sources include fortified foods such as non-dairy milks, margarine and breakfast cereals
Calcium	Textbooks state an additional 550mg/day to 1250mg/day per day. However, calcium absorption may increase at this time and compensate for increased needs. Nevertheless, as a precautionary measure, extra calcium rich foods should be taken	Green leafy vegetables, tahini, figs and almonds are the main sources and fortified non-dairy milks and fortified cereals may be considered
Zinc	Additional 6mg/day to 13mg/day	Wholegrains, nuts#, pulses, tofu, peas, parsley
Selenium	Additional 15mcg/day to 75mcg/day	Nuts#, bananas, soya beans, mushrooms and grains
Magnesium	Additional 50mmol/day to 320mmol/day.	Widespread in foods – wholegrains, nuts#, soya and yeast extracts
Iodine	140mcg/day. No increment needed during breastfeeding	Sea vegetables, kelp tablets and Vecon

Avoid nuts if there is a family history of allergy or atopic disorder
* Higher than Department of Health value

Farley's Soya Formula is the only formula feed suitable for vegan infants. Other soya formulas are unsuitable due to the vitamin D content that is derived from lanolin. Infant formula is an artificially manufactured milk that has been modified to make it more digestible for a young baby. Therefore, an ordinary non-dairy milk is not suitable as a sole feed for babies because it does not contain the appropriate nutrients.

The safety of soya-based infant formula has recently been called into question due to the wide review of evidence of the health risks and benefits of chemicals called phytoestrogens. These oestrogen-containing compounds that naturally occur in foods such as soya, may mimic or disrupt hormones in our bodies. The media recently took a study[5] out of context and stated that soya infant formula could harm sexual development and fertility as adults. This study looked at the reproductive health of young women who had soya formula as infants. The study concluded "our findings are reassuring about the safety of infant soya formula" which has been used for over 30 years. The UK Scientific Advisory Committee concluded that this study did not prove harm to human infants but recommended further studies were carried out[6].

There is no reputable scientific evidence to show that there are any adverse effects on infants who are fed soya infant formulas. Soya infant formulas have been fed to millions of babies worldwide and soya infant formula does not seem to lead to different general health or reproductive outcomes than exposure to cow's milk formula. We all know that "breast is best" but where breastfeeding is not possible, soya infant formula can be safely used.

Feed requirements
As with breastfed infants, bottle fed infants should be fed on demand. All infants are different and requirements may vary. As a guide, approximately 150-200ml per kg body weight per day should be offered in four to eight feeds. For example, a 4kg baby will need 600-800ml of feed, which may be six feeds of 100-130ml bottles.

It is important to follow the manufacturers' instructions when making the feed. If feeds are too concentrated your baby is likely to become constipated. The standard dilution of powdered infant feeds in the UK is one level scoop to each 30ml (1 fl oz) of measured water. Always use the scoop provided with the product.

Dental implications of soya infant formula
Another controversy surrounding the use of soya formulas is that the energy content is based on glucose syrup rather than lactose (milk sugar) and it has been thought to have a greater potential to contribute to dental caries than cow's milk formulas. No studies have shown that soya infant formula is any more harmful to teeth than dairy infant formula. Feeds from a bottle, feeding at bedtime, prolonged sucking, may be the most important factors in predicting caries development[7]. If normal weaning practices are adopted (see 'Drinks' on page 52) infant formulas should not cause harm to teeth. Soya infant formula has been used for more than 30 years and is comparable to dairy infant formula for safety and nutritional completeness. Remember, soya isn't a natural food for babies but neither is cow's milk which contains animal oestrogens - little is known about their effect on children!

When bottle feeding, do not allow prolonged or frequent contact of milk feeds with your baby's teeth since this increases the risk of tooth decay. As soon as the first tooth erupts (usually appears any time between 6 and 12 months although they may come through sooner or later than this) brush twice daily. Make sure your baby's teeth are cleaned after the last feed at night and try to wean your baby off the bottle by the age of one.

SUPPLEMENTS

If breastfeeding, you need to ensure a reliable daily source of vitamin B12, 4mcg from fortified foods or 10mcg from a supplement. Whilst breastfeeding, no other supplements are necessary for baby up to six months, providing mum has a good diet. Bottle fed babies do not need supplements as long as they consume more than 500ml (1 pint) of infant formula per day.

Once weaning begins, you need to provide your child with a daily source of 1mcg of vitamin B12, either through a supplement or with fortified foods. A powdered form of B12 is available that can be sprinkled on food.

From the age of six months up to five years of age, the Department of Health recommends all infants take supplements of vitamins A, C and D; these are available from the health visitor or at the chemist. These vitamins are known as 'welfare drops', suitable for vegans and in certain circumstances are available free of charge. There are differing views on whether babies actually need vitamin drops or not. They are really a safeguard to protect your infant through times of illness or faddy eating, when food intake may be inadequate. If your baby is well, takes a mixed diet and gets outside to top up vitamin D stores, then she probably doesn't need any supplementary vitamins. If your baby is consuming more than 500ml of infant formula per day, supplements are not needed because the formula is already fortified with vitamins.

GROWTH

The birth weight of infants born to vegan parents has been shown to be no different to infants born to non-vegan parents. All babies can lose up to 0.5kg (1lb) in the first few days of birth. This is normal. In those crucial early days, weight measurement is not very helpful in determining feeding success. It is quite normal for babies to lose up to 10% of their birth weight and they may start putting it back on only slowly.

Babies do vary in how fast they put on weight but as a rough guide, most breastfed babies will gain 4-5oz (100-125g) per week in the first three months and by six months most babies double their birth weight and treble it by a year. You can have your baby regularly weighed and checked at your local health clinic. Infants under six months of age should not be weighed more than once every 14 days and infants over six months not more than once per month.

At the clinic your baby's growth will be recorded on a centile chart (see overleaf). It doesn't matter where your baby starts on the chart. The chart is to plot her progress which should be fairly steady growth over a period of time.

Compared to formula fed infants, breastfed infants generally gain weight at about the same rate for the first two to three months and then gain weight less rapidly from 3-12 months[8]. This means by 12 months, breastfed infants will tend to be leaner than formula fed infants. At around three months babies commonly have a growth spurt which may result in an increased demand for milk feeds at this time and may only last a couple of days. Don't be tempted to begin weaning when this happens.

Infants born pre-term are nutritionally vulnerable. Particular attention is needed to ensure their energy and nutrient needs are met. Monitoring of growth is important and if you experience any difficulties with feeding, contact your paediatrician.

There is no one ideal rate of growth. Instead height, weight and head circumference are reported in percentiles. The average or ideal growth, according to the method, would be to fall on the 50th centile. This simply means if your child's height is at the 50th centile, 50% of children at that age are taller and 50% are shorter. Similarly a weight at the 25th centile means 25% of children weigh less and 75% weigh more. These growth charts can make parents anxious and yet we cannot say whether a child growing at the 25th centile is any more or less healthy than the child at the 75th centile.

Another factor affecting the child's growth is genetics. If the child is born to tall vegan parents, then the child is likely to be tall. The majority of vegan children are well within the acceptable range of height and weight for their age and studies have shown vegan children to be as strong as their peers and many with above average intelligence[9].

Vegan babies tend to be lighter in weight than their peers but heights tend to be average[10]. However, it should be remembered that these standard growth charts are based on meat eating children who generally show a more rapid growth pattern. The Child Growth Foundation suggest rapid infant weight gain may not be a good thing and recent studies suggest that larger, rapid growing children are more susceptible to diabetes[2] and other chronic diseases[11]. Therefore, the lighter vegan child may have a distinct advantage over her omnivore peers. However, it is important that the child is not underweight.

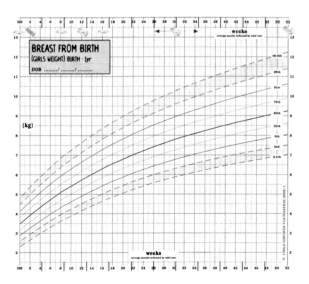

References from chapter 4

1 American Dietetic Association (ADA) (1997) *Promotion of breastfeeding* J Am Diet Assoc 97 662-666

2 Dahlquist G & Mustonen L (2000) *Analysis of 20 years of prospective registration of childhood onset diabetes time trends and birth cohort effects* Swedish Childhood Diabetes Study Group Acta Paediatr Oct 90(10)123-7

3 Specker BL Miller D Norman EJ Greene T Hayes KC (1988) *Methylmalonic acid excretion in breastfed infants of vegetarian mothers and identification of an acceptable dietary source of vitamin B12* Am J Clin Nutr 47 89-92

4 Voigt RG Jensen CL Fraley JK Rozelle JC Brown FR Heird WC (2002) *Relationship between omega 3 long chain polyunsaturated fatty acid status during early infancy and neurodevelopmental status at 1 year* J Hum Nutr Diet Apr 15(2) 111-20

5 Strom BL Schinnar R Ziegler E Barnhart K et al (2001) *Exposure to soy-based formula in infancy and endocrinological and reproductive outcomes in young adulthood* JAMA 286 807-814

6 COT (Committee on toxicity of Chemicals in Food, Consumer Products & the Environment) (2003) *Phytoestrogens and health* The Food Standards Agency London

7 Moyniham PJ et al (1996) *A comparison of the relative acidogenic potential of infant milk and soya infant formula: a plaque pH study* Int J Paed Dent 6(3) 177-181

8 Dewey KG et al (1995) *Growth of breast fed infants deviates from current reference data: a pooled analysis of US, Canadian and European Data Sets* Pediatrics 96 495-503

9 Sanders TAB Manning J (1992) *Growth and development of vegan children* J Hum Nutr Diet 5 11-21

Ellis FR et al (1970) *Veganism Clinical Findings and Investigations* Am J Clin Nutr 23 (3) 249

10 Sanders TAB Purves R (1981) *An anthropometric and dietary assessment of the nutritional status of vegan preschool children* J Hum Nutr 35 349-357

11 Heinig MJ et al (1993) *Energy and protein intakes of breastfed and bottle fed infants during the first year of life and their association with growth velocity: the DARLING Study* Am J Clin Nutr 58 152-61

Weaning

Breast milk provides all your baby needs for the first six months of her life. Therefore if your baby is happy and thriving, there is no need to think about introducing any solids until she is six months old[1]. After this time babies start to need more iron and their digestive systems become able to cope with a wider range of foods. The introduction of solid foods also helps with the development of chewing and biting.

Weaning is a gradual process that begins when you start to replace milk with solid foods. Solid foods should not be introduced before 17 weeks. After six months babies need more nutrients in their diet as breast or formula milk can no longer provide enough.

Your baby's calorie needs increase as she becomes more active and energetic and continues to grow. Weaning is often an anxious time for parents, with many viewing it with apprehension. This can be made worse by comments from anxious friends and relatives who question whether a vegan diet is suitable. However, the weaning process is really a very simple one and most babies accomplish it smoothly and you can be totally assured that a vegan diet offers all the nourishment your baby needs for growth and development. Weaning is a once in a lifetime opportunity to introduce eating habits that will keep your child healthy in the years to come.

Will weaning onto a vegan diet provide all the nutrients my baby needs?
Yes! The first recommended weaning foods for all babies are animal free – baby rice, pureed fruits and vegetables. As baby progresses onto a varied diet, the nutrients that frequently raise concerns are vitamin D, calcium and vitamin B12. However, these concerns are unfounded as with a little planning, these nutrients can be readily provided by the vegan diet[2].

How about dairy?
In the West, dairy products are assumed to be an essential part of a child's diet, encouraged because of the high amounts of protein, fat, carbohydrate and calcium that they provide. However, with the increase in obesity and other childhood complaints such as asthma, eczema, ear infections and most recently, childhood diabetes, some doctors and health professionals are questioning the role that dairy products play in our children's diet. The Department of Health recommend that whole cow's milk should not be introduced as a drink before a child is one year of age. The levels of protein, sodium and potassium in whole cows' milk may be too high for the infant's developing system to handle[3].

How can you tell when your baby is ready?
All babies are different. Some start solid food earlier, some later. Some take to it quickly, some take longer. Some are choosy, others like anything and everything. Six months is the recommended age for the introduction of solid foods. Whilst infants can be offered foods at an earlier age than six months, their developing systems are unable to cope. Be guided by what your baby seems to want. Starting solids is in any case a gradual process. In addition, there is the danger that introducing solids too early to an immature system can lead to allergies and food intolerances.

At around three months babies commonly have a growth spurt which may result in an increased demand for milk feeds at this time and may only last a couple of days. Don't be tempted to begin weaning when this happens.

Give solid foods a try when your baby

- still seems hungry after finishing a good milk feed and you have tried giving more milk

- starts to demand feeds more often

- maybe after sleeping through the night starts waking again to be fed

- seems more restless than usual

- is six months old

She may appear more restless after feeds, as if your baby was asking for something more. At this time, babies start to show an interest in other foods, they begin to explore the taste and texture of just about anything.

FIRST FOODS

Interestingly, suitable first weaning foods for all babies are vegan and include baby rice and pureed vegetables and fruit (see weaning timetable) but remember that breast and formula milk is still an important source of nutrition and can be added to weaning foods to make the taste more familiar. The first foods offered should be gluten free – gluten is found in wheat, rye, barley and oats. Because a small number of infants can't cope with gluten, it is best to wait until the baby is six months old. Certain foods are thought better left until later on because the young digestive system may be too immature to cope with them or because these foods may be linked with the development of food allergies or intolerances if introduced too early.

Many parents worry about possible allergic reactions when introducing the baby to new foods. Allergies are quite rare and where they do occur they are usually inherited so you will know in advance if they are likely. Common reactions include skin rashes or sore bottoms.

What you need

- A plastic sieve is useful for preparing fruit or vegetables. After cooking, force fruits and vegetables through the sieve with the back of a spoon to get rid of any lumps.

- Alternatively, a hand blender or an electric blender saves time and is easier to use.

- A baby spoon – these spoons are plastic and softer, smaller and flatter than adult spoons

- Ice cube trays and freezer bags – put food into ice cube trays, freeze it and then put the frozen cubes of food into freezer bags. These can then be used as needed

First foods need to be

- just a little thicker than milk

- smooth in texture

- bland in flavour

- free from artificial flavourings

- free from sugar and salt

The recommended order in which foods should be eaten

 baby rice
 ▼
pureed root vegetables: potatoes, carrots, parsnips, swedes, turnip
 ▼
pureed fruit: apple, pear, banana, peaches (not citrus until nine months)
 ▼
other vegetables: peas, beans, lentils
 ▼
other cereals (gluten foods after six months)

Start with a little vegetable purée or rice cereal on the tip of a flat shallow spoon or your finger (see Weaning Timetable on pages 41-42 for order in which to introduce foods). The first few spoonfuls are just to get your baby used to the taste and feel of solid food. How much your baby takes is less important than getting used to the idea of food other than milk. You can go on breastfeeding your baby alongside giving solid food for as long as desired. A bedtime breastfeed can make a good end to the day. Continuing breastfeeding during the first year and beyond ensures a good source of nutrients. Remember, now you are weaning your infant you need to provide her with a reliable regular source of vitamin B12 fortified foods or sprinkle 1mcg of B12 powder daily into baby's food.

First week

Breast or bottle feed as you and your baby are used to with a small teaspoon of baby rice offered at lunchtime. It should be smooth and fairly runny, making it easy for the food to be taken from the spoon. Make sure your baby is in a sitting position when eating.

Try to follow your baby's appetite. Just a small teaspoon is enough at first. Be prepared for her to spit out your offerings. Don't press the food on your baby. Most babies take time to learn how to take food from a spoon.

Your baby may also cry between mouthfuls at first and may push the food out but she is experimenting with the texture and taste and this is quite natural. Until now, food has come in one continuous stream, now there are frustrating pauses. Don't force the food, if it really doesn't seem wanted, leave it a day or two or maybe a week and then try again. Don't add solid food to bottle feeds as it can cause choking.

Preferably give the solid food before the milk feed so as time goes on you can gradually increase the quantity until the baby is satisfied. Once starting solid food, some people believe you need to stop breastfeeding. There is no need to wean your baby from the breast completely unless you wish to. Continue breastfeeding for as long as you wish. If it works better, offer the weaning food in the middle of the milk feed, there is no point in trying to give solids if the baby is hungry, wanting comfort and crying for a feed. Better to give a milk feed first and give the solids afterwards. This means your baby will be calm and happy, with the edge taken off any hunger or thirst before the more unfamiliar food is given. You can then finish off the meal with the rest of the milk feed. However if your baby still likes to go to sleep after a milk feed, giving all of it before the solids may not be a good idea as she may be too tired to be bothered with anything else.

For atopic (allergic) babies, it is a good idea to try your baby on the same food for several days before introducing another so you can make sure there is no allergic response.

Here's a suggested 'timetable' for a baby just starting on solid food

	During first week of weaning	After one week of weaning
Breakfast	Breast or infant milk	Pureed vegetables Breast or infant milk
Lunch	Baby rice mixed with breast or infant milk plus feed	Baby rice mixed with breast or infant milk plus feed
Tea	Breast or infant milk	Fruit or vegetable purée and breast or infant milk
Late evening	Breast or infant milk	Breast or infant milk

Second week

You may offer, for example, pureed vegetable at lunch time and apple with rice at tea time. Go at your baby's pace. If your baby is keen, you can give larger amounts. Keep up your usual milk feeds. Your baby may drop a milk feed if she's been feeding often. Begin to add different foods and different tastes, but take it slowly. Two or three new foods each week is probably fast enough. You may be able to use lots of the foods you already cook for yourself – just purée a small amount (without added sugar or salt).

Third week

Once your baby has grown used to a variety of foods, you can begin to give the solids first and the milk second. Give a small amount of rice cereal at breakfast time. Try a different vegetable at lunch time. Fruit and rice at teatime as before. Breast or bottle feeds as before.

Fourth week

During the next few weeks, gradually make the food a thicker consistency. Make vegetable purees more substantial – combine potato, yam or parsnip with other vegetables and try a different fruit with the baby rice. One breast or bottle feed at tea time or lunch time could be swapped for a drink of fortified non-dairy milk or water from a cup. By now your baby is having three small meals a day plus extra fortified non-dairy milk. Try to match the portion size to your baby's appetite. Work towards offering three meals at a time that fits in with when you eat, so you and your baby can enjoy eating together.

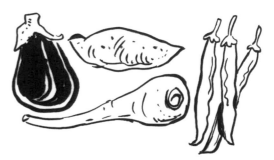

WEANING TIMETABLE

Not before 17 weeks Pureed foods – learning to eat from a spoon	*Iron fortified rice cereal*	Mix with breast milk or formula milk
	Vegetables: carrot, swede, courgette, plantain, yam, turnip, sweet potatoes, potatoes, green beans, parsnip, pumpkin (remove the seeds)	Scrub or peel vegetables as necessary and steam until tender. Purée with enough cooking water or milk to make a soft consistency. Start by giving ½ tspn before or after the midday or evening milk. Some of the stronger flavoured vegetables eg turnip and parsnip may go down better if blended with a little mashed potato. To preserve nutrients, cook with the skin on and then remove before serving to avoid an excess of fibre which may provide too much bulk
Breast or formula milk is still the most important source of nutrition. However, if you wish to, weaning can be started by introducing a ½ teaspoon of baby rice or pureed vegetables or fruit after or before a milk feed once a day		
Your baby still needs breast milk or about 600ml (1 pint) of infant milk each day	*Avocado*	Scoop out and mash a little of the flesh, adding a few drops of boiled water or milk to soften if necessary
	Fruit: bananas, pears, apples	Purée fruit. Use sweet apples only
After six months[#] Learning to eat lumps and pieces	Lentils Non-dairy milks	It is now time to move from purees to mashed or minced food. Offer your baby several small meals each day. Slowly introduce a wider range of foods
	Soft fruits eg, melon, mango	
Your baby will generally want less milk as more solids are taken *Try some first finger foods*[^] *Try giving some drinks from a cup* *You can now introduce wheat and oats*	Dried fruits: dates Vegetables: spinach, broccoli, brussel sprouts, cabbage	
	Pulses: lentils Grains: corn meal, sago and millet, wheat and oats	Cook until soft and mushy
	Seeds*	Smooth sesame seed or tahini spreads provide useful quantities of calcium, minerals and calories and can be added to meals eg mashed potatoes

Weaning timetable continued

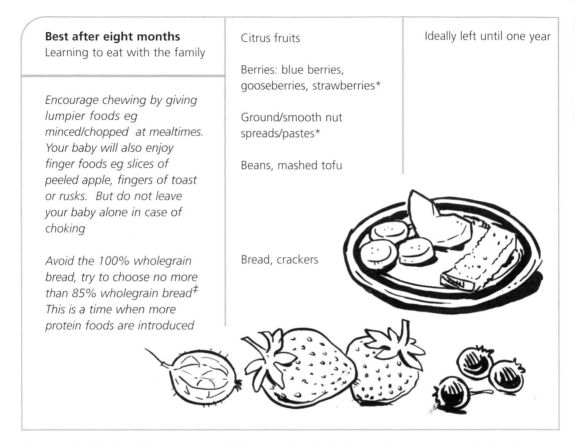

Best after eight months Learning to eat with the family	Citrus fruits	Ideally left until one year
Encourage chewing by giving lumpier foods eg minced/chopped at mealtimes. Your baby will also enjoy finger foods eg slices of peeled apple, fingers of toast or rusks. But do not leave your baby alone in case of choking *Avoid the 100% wholegrain bread, try to choose no more than 85% wholegrain bread‡ This is a time when more protein foods are introduced*	Berries: blue berries, gooseberries, strawberries* Ground/smooth nut spreads/pastes* Beans, mashed tofu Bread, crackers	

If there is a family history of allergy avoid nuts until three years of age. Seeds, berries and soya can cause an allergic reaction.

#*at weaning it is essential to include a reliable daily source of vitamin B12 either with fortified foods or crush a tablet into baby's food.*

‡*The bran in 100% wholemeal bread may be too laxative for some infants.*

^ *Take care to supervise as some babies can easily choke*

WEANING STAGES
Not before 17 weeks

Try to make your own baby foods rather than relying on manufactured products. These should be prepared without added sugar, salt or spices. Rice is the best first cereal to choose. Ideally choose one fortified with vitamins and minerals. Vegetables may be introduced next.

You might find it handy to freeze small quantities of pureed vegetables in ice cube trays or small pots with lids and transfer them to plastic bags. Then take just one or two pieces as you need them, defrost and reheat.

If you are not using the food immediately, cover, cool quickly and store in the fridge until the next meal. Vegetables should be pureed – carrot, swede, courgette, plantain, yam, turnip, sweet potatoes, potatoes, green beans or parsnip are good first vegetables. You can add a little beetroot juice to mashed potato – it goes a lovely pink colour and is popular with infants (see Appendix for weaning recipes).

Scrub or peel vegetables as necessary and steam until tender, approximately 10-15 minutes. Cook whole to preserve vitamins and minerals but remove skins before serving to avoid too much bulk. Purée with enough cooking water or milk to make a soft consistency. If there are any lumps, push the food through a sieve. Start by giving half a teaspoon before or after the midday or evening milk. Fruits are usually introduced after vegetables in order to allow acceptance of vegetables before the sweet taste of fruits is experienced. Good first fruits are pureed bananas, pears or peaches. Avoid fruit with seeds and pips unless you can remove them first.

It may take a week or two before your baby has got the hang of using a spoon. Remember, the first few weeks are just to get your baby used to the taste and texture of solid foods. These first tastes of solid food are just that and are not meant to provide lots of nourishment.

After six months

Try giving some drinks from a cup. You can now begin introducing other cereals such as oats, wheat, barley and corn. Encourage chewing by giving lumpier foods at mealtimes. Your baby will also enjoy finger foods which are an important if messy stage of baby's development. Once your baby can hold and handle things, try giving soft finger foods but remember never leave baby alone when eating. This gives good chewing practice and it will help your baby to learn to feed herself.

Suitable finger foods include banana, pear, melon and mango slices. Make sure you remove skin and pips from all fruit. Avoid foods like sweet biscuits so your baby doesn't get into the habit of expecting sweet snacks. Finely milled seeds eg pumpkin, sesame, sunflower can be stirred into fruit or vegetable purees and lentil dishes. Just add half a teaspoon to start with. Some parents may wish to give toast or crackers as finger foods but take care, some children may easily choke and these therefore are best delayed until 8 months.

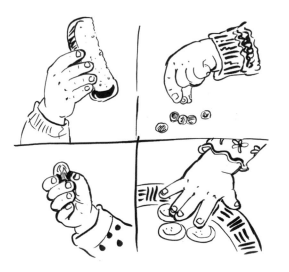

Summary

- Breastfeeding provides all the nutrition your baby needs for up to the first six months of life

- Solids should not be introduced before 17 weeks

- Do not rush to give solids before six months

- By six months your baby needs more than just milk

- Breastfeeding and infant formula can be continued up to two years and beyond

Moving on
After eight months

At this stage your vegan baby can have just about anything! This stage is marked by a move to three meals a day (see menu idea). Citrus fruit and fruit juices can now be introduced – they are common allergens and if you can delay introducing until after your child's first birthday, this is preferable. Each day try to give your baby foods from each of the five food groups (see plate model on pages 4-5) and you can now combine lots of textures and flavours.

Protein foods are generally introduced around eight months and good sources of protein include mashed cooked beans, lentils, tofu and soya yoghurt. When introducing beans, check the baby's stool to see whether the beans are being digested well. If the stool smells sour, if the baby's bottom becomes reddened or irritated, or if parts of beans are seen, wait a while before trying beans again. Some children do not tolerate whole beans until age two or three years. Other grains and soya products will meet your child's nutritional needs.

Menu idea

**** *Early morning* ****
Breastmilk or infant formula

**** *Breakfast* ****
Cereal with non-dairy milk, two or three toast fingers and diluted pure fruit juice

**** *Lunch* ****
Lentil and vegetable hotpot
Stewed fruit and soya custard
Juice

**** *Tea* ****
Banana and tahini sandwich, fresh fruit and breastmilk

**** *Bedtime* ****
Breastmilk or infant formula

Tips

- Fruit can be fresh, tinned, cooked or raw. Remove any peel or pips before giving the food to your baby

- Unsalted vegetables from family meals can be used. Peel the vegetables and use the cooking water or milk for pureeing

- Freeze vegetable sticks such as carrots and cucumber – a teething baby will love chewing on these

- Make a family meal which can also be given to baby eg pasta, rice pudding

Your baby's brain is still developing very rapidly at this time. To help development, try including foods that contain w-3 fatty acids as the body is unable to make these on its own. Good sources are rapeseed (canola), flaxseed (linseed), hempseed and walnut oils.

When your baby begins to chew, you will only have to chop up food. Finger foods continue to be an important part of meal times. If your baby is a good chewer, offer sticks of raw vegetables: carrots, swede, celery, cauliflower and fruit such as apple slices – these may need to be lightly cooked if baby has no teeth.

Finger food suggestions
Cooked vegetables, yam, plantain, beetroot, cooked peas, sweetcorn, slices of pepper or mushroom and cucumber. Mango, banana, pear, plum, peach, apricot and kiwi fruit (make sure it is peeled and any pips removed). Cooked pasta shapes, vegan sausages (some are solid enough for your child to feed herself) bread and toast fingers spread with a little margarine, smooth peanut butter or tahini, and breadsticks. Rice cakes or fingers of wholemeal bread baked in the oven until hard make good replacements for sugar rusks.

Encourage your child to appreciate raw vegetables like carrots and cucumbers. Grate them finely or try putting a dab of peanut butter, tahini or almond butter on these vegetables which will often entice a child. Plain tofu, rice cakes and nori (seaweed strips) are other healthful snacks. Most children love noodles and pasta with vegetables served with gravies and sauces, these can provide extra energy and protein.

MANUFACTURED BABY FOOD
Some parents choose to use commercial baby foods. Tins or jars of baby food can be useful but don't let them replace home-made food altogether. There are products made for vegetarian babies that are suitable for the vegan infant but careful label reading is recommended. A list of suitable brands of vegan baby foods and other baby products can be found in *The Animal Free Shopper*, available from The Vegan Society, or contact the food companies directly.

If you do give your baby bought foods, try to mix with fresh foods. Always check foods are suitable for your baby's age. Choose brands without added sugars or sweeteners. The added sugars to avoid are glucose, glucose syrup, honey, dextrose, sucrose, invert syrup and maltose. If you don't use all the contents of the packet at one meal, store in the fridge but use up within 24 hours. Never reheat food for your baby; if it has been heated once but not eaten, throw it away. Never put the spoon you've used for feeding into the jar you plan to store for another meal because of the risk of contamination.

When reading labels it isn't always clear whether an ingredient is derived from animals. Ingredients such as butter, animal fat and lard are recognisable as unsuitable products. Other ingredients are not as clear. See page 65 for a brief example of some common animal derived ingredients to be avoided. For a more comprehensive list and a guide to which products are suitable to buy, see *The Animal Free Shopper*.

IS MY CHILD GETTING ENOUGH ENERGY?
Concern has been expressed that infants and young children may have trouble obtaining sufficient energy on a vegan diet. If the diet is mixed and varied and your child is fed at regular intervals through the day there is no reason why energy intake should be low.

You may find it hard to tell how much food to give, but the best guide is your baby's appetite.

Rigid feeding regimes are unnecessary, especially if a baby is still breastfed. If your child is growing normally and appears happy and well, it is likely that she is getting enough nutrition. Do not restrict dietary fat in children younger than two years. Fat is the major source of energy and breast and bottle milk contribute approximately 50% of energy as fat. As your child progresses, the proportion of energy from fat decreases from 50% to 35% energy and is replaced by carbohydrate but adequate energy (calories) is needed for growth. Ensure that you are not providing too much bulk by including energy dense, high calorie foods such as mashed avocado, vegetable oil and nut and seed butters, perhaps peeling vegetables and fruit to help meet nutrient and energy needs. As a guide, a seven to nine month old will need solids three to four times per day with breast milk, formula or fortified non-dairy milk. From nine to twelve months of age, feed solids five to six times per day. Never add sugar or salt to your baby's food, even if it tastes bland to you. Infants learn to like foods that they are given at an early age.

FIRST DRINKS

Up to the age of six months exclusive breastfeeding is recommended[4] or formula milk is the only drink most babies need. Offering drinks other than breast or formula feed may reduce the babies appetite for milk feeds. On hot summer days you may find your baby needs more breastfeeds. You may have been encouraged to give your baby drinks of water early on but this is not necessary and giving water could disturb your supply of breast milk. Unless you really feel your baby needs a drink, you don't need to offer her anything other than milk until the age of six months. Try to continue to offer breast milk for as long as possible.

Bottled mineral water is not suitable for infants as it may contain high mineral contents. Avoid the carbonated (fizzy) varieties as they are acidic and your baby can fill up with gas. Water is a very underrated drink for the whole family and tap water is safe and kind to teeth. Once solids are established cooled boiled tap water can be given alongside a milk feed. All drinks that contain sugar, however little, or fruit juices (containing natural sugar) can be harmful to teeth if drunk frequently. If you wish to give a flavoured drink, unsweetened diluted fruit juice is best – dilute one part juice to ten parts water. As your child grows older, from one year, you may wish to dilute less – one part juice to five parts water.

The Department of Health do not recommend cow's milk before the age of six months and only small amounts up to 12 months of age. The common habit of giving cow's milk as the main drink at an early age can prejudice iron status and is relatively low in vitamin D. Giving cows milk as

a drink with a meal or mixing milk with solid foods can reduce absorption of iron[5]. Breast milk and/or infant formula should be the main drinks in the diet throughout the first year of life. Non-dairy milks can be included in the diet at weaning but try to choose those higher in fat and fortified with vitamins and calcium.

You can start giving drinks from a cup with a spout when you begin weaning. A cup without a lid is the best choice. This type of cup is best because it encourages your baby to develop a sipping action when drinking. Infants love to do things for themselves and will enjoy holding a beaker and using a spoon to feed themselves.

Plain non-dairy milk (without any added sweeteners) or water are the only safe drinks for teeth. Once you have started to introduce a beaker, you should begin to reduce the use of a bottle or dummy. Start by removing them whenever possible during the day. Then restrict them to bedtime, and remove as soon as your baby is asleep.

As your baby eats more food, the amount of milk taken will go down. Encourage drinks at mealtime rather than making drinks continually available. By a year you should aim for five to six small (200ml) cups per day. If she drinks less than this she may become constipated. If she drinks a lot more, she may not be interested in food.

FOODS TO AVOID AND FOOD ALLERGIES

Certain foods are thought better left until later on. This is because they may be difficult for a young digestive system to cope with or because they are considered to be linked with the development of food allergies or intolerance if introduced too early. These include cereals, citrus fruits (eg oranges, grapefruit), nuts and strong tasting vegetables such as chillies. Honey is unsuitable for vegans and should be avoided in all infants. It may

contain spores which could cause a serious infection called botulism.

The most common foods which are associated with food allergy are cow's milk, eggs, fish, shellfish, peanuts, nuts, gluten containing cereals and soya. Cow's milk is the commonest cause of childhood allergies and in the UK it is estimated that around 6% of children under the age of five years are affected. A food allergy is a reaction to an otherwise harmless food or food component that involves the body's immune (defence) system. A reaction occurs when the body's immune system responds abnormally to the protein or proteins in that particular food. The body reacts by flooding the system with histamine and other chemicals to fight off what is perceived as an invader in the body. Reactions to food or food ingredients that do not involve the immune system are called a food intolerance or sensitivity and these are less dramatic with slower reactions.

Although the popular press report that 20-30% of the population is affected by food allergy, there is evidence that food allergy affects 1-2% of the general population and 5-8% of children. Many children with food allergy grow out of it by the time they start school. For those with allergy, the problem must be taken seriously. Around 2-3% of children suffer with cow's milk protein allergy.

If there is a family history of allergies or atopic (skin) disorders, there is an increased likelihood of children being allergic. If an infant or child has other food allergies or has a family history of food or other allergies, withholding introduction of peanuts until after three years of age has been recommended[6]. Studies in the UK have shown no detectable protein in refined peanut oil. This is because the process of refining oil removes peanut protein which is responsible for triggering an allergic reaction. Peanuts may be a particular problem because they contain a protein which can cause the lining of the lung to swell. Peanut oil (sometimes labelled as groundnut oil) is commonly used as a component in vegetable oil, as a carrier in processed foods or as an emulsifier/lubricant in cosmetics. Oils which are cold pressed to retain their flavour or oil that has been used to cook peanuts do contain peanut protein and therefore should be avoided.

Weaning a child before 17 weeks of age increases the risk of allergy – see the weaning timetable on pages 41-42 to guide you as to which foods should be introduced first to prevent any risk of allergy. For example, wheat should not be among the first weaning foods introduced into the child's diet and ideally should be introduced after eight months of age.

Don't add artificial sweetener or salt to your baby's food. Too much salt is bad for the kidneys and could lead to dehydration. Foods which taste quite bland to you may be an exciting new experience for your baby. If buying convenience foods, try to avoid those with added salt.

Sugar

Try to avoid adding sugar to foods. This can encourage a sweet tooth and lead to tooth decay later on. Children get used to the sweet taste.

Vegan children have been shown to have good teeth with a low level of dental caries which may be due to less added sugar in the diet[7]. However, all sugars (including the sugar in fruit and fruit juices) and sugary foods can be used by bacteria in the mouth to make acid which can attack the teeth and lead to tooth decay. This can also happen with some starchy foods and savoury snacks. However teeth can cope with about three meals and two to three snacks a day if they are regularly brushed. Sugary and acidic foods and drinks are best included at meal times rather than intermittently through the day. Sugar contains few nutrients. Dried and fresh fruit, natural fruit juices and no added sugar jams are a healthier source of sweetness in the diet.

If wishing to sweeten puddings with sugar, use it sparingly. The only sugar that offers any significant nutrition is blackstrap molasses which contains calcium and iron.

Choking

Toddlers and pre-schoolers are at increased risk of choking because they are still learning to chew and swallow. They may not have a full set of teeth and they may not want to take the time to chew food fully. Children under five can choke on any small object.

The following points will help reduce the risk of choking:

- Only choose smooth, not crunchy, nut butters

- Be careful with finger foods such as hard sticks of vegetables or fruit

- Cherry tomatoes and grapes should be halved

- Popcorn should be avoided

- Avoid whole or chopped nuts

If your baby chokes, don't waste time trying to remove the object from her mouth unless it can be done easily. Turn your baby, head down,

supporting her body with your forearm and slap firmly between the shoulder blades. If your baby is older lay her over your lap and slap firmly between the shoulder blades [8].

SUPPLEMENTS

Once weaning begins, you need to provide your child with a vitamin B12 supplement of 1mcg per day if the diet does not contain enough fortified foods. Vitamin B12 is available in powder form and is very palatable. It can be taken straight from a teaspoon or sprinkled on food. Several supplements are available from health food shops or local pharmacists. Apart from vitamin B12, a varied diet should be able to provide all the nutrients needed for growth and development. However the Department of Health recommends all infants take supplements of vitamin A, D and C up to five years of age[9]. These are available from your Health Visitor or at a chemist. They are really just a safeguard (see page 34).

At one year of age you can start adding a regular source of w-3 fatty acids such as half a teaspoon of flaxseed oil – important for brain development. See pages 54-55.

Summary

■ Ensure a reliable, regular source of vitamin B12

■ Breast or formula milk should be the main drinks throughout the first year of life

■ Encourage her to eat with finger foods

■ By the time she is one year old she will get most of the goodness she needs from her foods. Drinks (including milk) should now be a smaller part

■ At one year of age, start adding a regular source of omega 3 fatty acids

References for chapter 5

1 American Dietetic Association (1997) *Promotion of breastfeeding* J Am Diet Assoc 97 662-666

2 Mangels AR Messina V (2001) *Considerations in planning vegan diets: infants* J American Dietetic Assoc 101(6) 670-677

3 Mangels AR Messina V Melina V (2003) *Position of the American Dietetic Assocation and Dietitians of Canada: Vegetarian Diets* J Am Diet Assoc 103 748-65

4 Butte NF Lopez-Alarcon MG Garza C (2002) *Nutrient adequacy of exclusive breastfeeding for the term infant during the first six months of life* WHO Geneva

5 Practice Nutrition (1995) *Diet and health in pre-school children* IBSN 0965-9722 Vol 4:2 July

6 Department of Health (1998) *Present day practice in infant feeding: third report* Report of a working party of the panel on child nutrition Committee on Medical Aspects of Food policy HMSO London

7 Sanders TAB Manning J (1992) *The growth and development of vegan children* JH Nutr & Diet 5 11-21

8 Health Education Authority (1992) *Play it Safe leaflet* Child Accident Prevention Trust, 28 Portland Place, London

9 COMA (1994) *Weaning and the Weaning Diet* Department of Health

The Older Infant

A GREAT START

By now you should be reassured that a vegan diet can provide all the nutrients needed for good health and has many health advantages but putting it into practice often raises concerns. Vegan toddlers have the same nutritional requirements as their non-vegan peers. By about one year of age your child is likely to be feeding herself. Some babies are very independent and want no help. Some vegan parents say their children, as with non-vegan children, have picky eating habits and a dislike of vegetables. However, the vegan diet often introduces a wider variety of foods. Most children are ready to join in with family meals by their first birthday, it just depends on your child's interest and how many teeth she has! If your baby has few teeth you will need to continue to finely chop and grind certain foods.

● Keep trying your baby with new foods; she may be less keen to try once she is over one year old

● Encourage her to join in with meals – provide a spoon and let her make a mess as this is the way she'll learn

● Provide food that can easily be picked up with fingers

Remember to avoid added salt and sugar and highly spiced foods. If you are eating healthily, this will also encourage your child to do so. Try to make the diet as varied as possible, with lots of colour and include plenty of finger foods. Popular finger food choices are bananas, peeled apple slices, breadsticks, chapatti or pitta bread, bread and toast fingers, cooked pasta shapes, raw or lightly steamed vegetables such as carrots, green beans and thin cut sandwich pieces.

Young children need three meals a day, plus two to three nutritional snacks. A regular source of vitamin B12 from fortified foods such as non-dairy milk, yeast extracts, TVP and breakfast cereals or vitamin B12 supplements should be used.

What shall I give her?

Encouraging children to eat well right from the start will have a positive impact on them in the future affecting health, weight and need for medical treatment. Unfortunately, with the mixed messages we hear from the media, obtaining accurate information on nutrition can present a challenge. However, be assured that the vegan diet can provide all the nutrients a growing child needs and such a diet can stand head and shoulders above the conventional diet of the western world.

Try to provide your child with a variety of foods (see introduction for more detailed information on food groups).

DRINKS

Try to wean your baby off the bottle by the age of one year. You don't have to use a lidded, spouted baby cup, an ordinary cup held up to her mouth is fine but a baby cup does mean she's probably able to drink without your help rather sooner. However, an open cup is best, even though it is messier. Start with this cup once a day and then offer it more often as she gets better at drinking from it. Plain water or non-dairy milk are the best drinks to offer. If you do offer juice, make sure you add water, diluting at least four to five parts of water to one part of juice (see pages 46-47 for further information on drinks).

PROVIDING ENOUGH NUTRITION

Toddlers and pre-schoolers often tend to eat less than most parents think they should. This is generally due to a developing sense of independence and a slow-down in growth. The pre-school years are an important time for developing healthy eating patterns which can set the stage for a healthful adult diet. Offering healthy foods at home, with the whole family involved in the preparation, helps the child take an interest in and learn tastes that can help them throughout life. Nevertheless, bringing up a child in a non-vegan world can be stressful. When your child starts attending nursery and generally socialising, you are likely to be questioned regarding your vegan diet and this can at times seem threatening and intrusive, particularly when it is from those who have little understanding of their own diet! However, treat this positively, as an opportunity to share your recipes and beliefs. This is very likely to generate surprise and an interest in your diet and lifestyle.

SUGGESTED MENU IDEAS FOR THE OLDER INFANT

**** Breakfast****
Wholemeal toast spread with margarine/peanut butter/tahini and yeast extract
Porridge made with non-dairy milk and dried fruit
Fresh fruit smoothie made with non-dairy milk and fruit of choice eg apricots, apple, banana
Scrambled tofu on toast
Rice cakes spread with tahini and mashed banana
Baked beans on toast
Cereal and milk
Banana and soya yoghurt

**** Snacks****
Fresh and dried fruit
Yoghurt
Nuts and seeds
Crispbreads/bagels/bread/pittas/crackers spread with tahini/nut butter/margarine/pâté
Homemade cakes eg flapjacks, fruit cake, scones, muffins

**** Lunch****
Sandwiches eg tahini and salad; tofu and watercress; banana and peanut butter
Veggie burger in bun with salad and beansprouts
Bean and vegetable soup with bread
Jacket potato and filling eg sweetcorn and tofu, beans and cucumber, soya cheese and tomato; hummus and watercress
Samosas/onion bhajis with salad
'Sausage' rolls
Tofu and salad sandwich
Toasted sandwiches: banana and peanut butter; tahini and tomato; yeast pâté and olives; 'cheese' and pickle

**** Tea****
Lasagne made with pasta/beans/tomato sauce and tofu topping
Spaghetti bolognaise made with pasta, TVP and pasta sauce
Bean and vegetable stew with dumplings
Nut roast and vegetables
Brown rice, tofu and vegetable stir fry
Pasta and broccoli with white sauce and tofu
Chick pea curry with vegetables and chapatti

**** Puddings****
Fresh fruit salad and custard
Fruit pie/crumble with soya cream or ice cream
Tofu and fresh fruit smoothie
Tapioca, semolina or rice pudding
Tofu cheesecake with fresh fruit
Scones with margarine and jam
Fruit cake

Many recommendations for nutrient intakes for infants and children by the Department of Health[1] have been extrapolated from data collected on adults as there was no suitable data for children. Therefore the dietary reference values (DRVs) should be used as a guide only. Listed below are some of the main nutrients that are often questioned when adopting a vegan diet.

Energy

Carbohydrates are the main energy foods. There are three types of carbohydrates: (1) sugars – sweets, cakes, biscuits, fruit (fresh or dried), added sugars (2) starches – bread, rice, pasta, potatoes (3) fibre – the indigestible part of vegetables or grains – essential for the digestive system to work properly and also protects against cancer. Carbohydrate foods should be consumed in as unrefined form as possible eg wholegrain breads, wholemeal pasta. Some form of carbohydrate should be provided at each meal. Try not to provide too many processed foods such as cakes and biscuits as they provide little in the way of nutrition apart from calories. If you are including sweet foods, healthier choices are fruit cakes and loaves, tea cakes, wholemeal scones or try to make your own cakes and biscuits adding in extra fruit, nuts and seeds in place of sugar. A diet rich in fresh fruits, vegetables and wholegrains should be encouraged. This diet is also high in fibre and may prove bulky. Therefore if you are concerned that your child is not getting enough calories (energy), reduce the amount of fibre in the diet by peeling fruits and vegetables and perhaps including less whole grains and including more refined grain products such as white flour and white rice. Adding half a teaspoon of flaxseed oil or one teaspoon of flaxseed powder per day to foods such as porridge will increase calorie content and provide essential fatty acids needed for brain growth and immune function. Including fruit juices, foods like avocado, nut and seed butters, dried fruits and soya products can provide a lot of calories in small quantities - ideal for the growing child.

Protein

Babies need a high intake of protein because they are growing very rapidly. From birth to six months the protein requirement is approximately one gram for every 0.5kg (1lb) of body weight each day. Protein is needed for growth, repair and replacement of cells in the body. Proteins are made up of building blocks called amino acids. The human body can manufacture only 14 of the 22 amino acids it needs, the other eight that must be supplied in the diet are called the 'essential' amino acids.

There is no need to worry about 'complementary proteins' or 'protein combining' to obtain these eight amino acids all at the same time as the body has a 'pool' of protein. Just ensure your child's daily diet is varied including at least one of the protein rich foods such as beans, nuts and pulses, soya foods, grains and seeds at each meal. Plant sources can provide adequate amounts of essential and non-essential amino acids. However, when dietary protein comes from plant foods it is about 85% digestible and to allow for this, the protein needs of vegan children may be slightly higher than non-vegan children[2]. Adequate protein intake is important for calcium status. So adding this extra protein to the Department of Health RNI's is recommended and can easily be met in a diet containing adequate calories (see table overleaf).

So be assured, a child will easily meet protein needs if a variety of plant foods are eaten and calorie intake is adequate. The majority of

Protein requirements

Age	Average weight (kg)	Recommended nutrient intake (RNI) for omnivores (g/day)	Recommended intake for vegans (g/day)
1-3 years	12.5	14.5	17.4-18.9
4-6 years	17.8	19.7	23.6-25.6
7-10 years	38.4	28.3	32.5-34.0

omnivores consume more protein than needed and it should be remembered that all foods contain some protein, be it in trace amounts. In fact, on a varied diet it would be very difficult to go short of protein without actually going short of food! Nevertheless, it is important to include a good source of protein at each meal.

Portions of foods containing 5g protein	
Brazils	35g (1½ oz)
Cashews	27g (1oz)
Lentils (cooked)	55g (2oz)
Sesame seeds	27g (1oz)
Soya cheese	100g (4oz)
Wholemeal bread	1½ slices (55g/2oz)
Dried apricots	125g (4oz)

Try to provide your child with several meals and snacks a day. Variety is the key to a healthy diet. Good sources of protein include pulses (peas, lentils, beans) grains (rice, pasta, oats, bread), soya products, nuts and seeds.

Well meaning omnivores may suggest that animal proteins are superior. The feeble logic of this argument is seen when you realize that these animals build up their proteins from plant sources anyway!

In fact soya protein has been shown to be nutritionally equivalent in protein value to proteins of animal origin and contains all the essential amino acids. A varied well planned plant diet ensures plenty of good quality protein with no shortage of any particular amino acid.

Fats

Children need a lot of energy in relation to their size and including fats in the diet helps to ensure adequate energy intake. During infancy there is rapid growth and fat is important for brain development. To meet the high need for calories during this time, children should not have any restriction of fat. For the older child (more than two years of age) there is a gradual reduction in fat from 50% to 35% of energy. Over five years of age, no more than 35% of calories should come from fat. Include foods such as nuts, seeds, soya products and avocados. Avoid foods containing hydrogenated fats (found in processed foods such as biscuits and pastries and some margarines). It is generally recognised that the general population consume too much fat, particularly saturated fat. In contrast, vegan diets more closely meet the UK Department of Health recommendations.

Omega 3 fatty acids

There are two types of fats; saturated and unsaturated. The saturated fats, mainly from animals, are not essential in the diet but the two fatty acids, linoleic (omega-6) and alpha-linolenic (omega-3), from polyunsaturated vegetable fats, are essential because they cannot be made by the body and need to be obtained from food. Vegan diets tend to have a high intake of the omega-6 polyunsaturated fatty acid, linoleic acid (LA) because it is in most plant foods compared with the omega-3 fatty acid, alpha linolenic acid (ALA) which is only found in a few foods. Although this has not been shown to be harmful, it is prudent to try to include more foods rich in omega-3 fatty acids. See table below for good sources of omega 3 fatty acids.

Essential Fatty Acids (polyunsaturated fatty acids)	
LINOLEIC (LA) (Omega 6 fatty acids) In vegetables, fruits, nuts, grains, seeds; corn, sunflower, soya, palm and peanut oils converted in the body to ▼	ALPHA LINOLENIC (ALA) (Omega 3 fatty acids) In flaxseeds, walnut and rapeseed oils, in green leafy vegetables and grains converted in the body to ▼
GLA (gamma-linolenic acid) In oils of blackcurrant, borage and evening primrose oil converted in the body to ▼	Eicosapentaenoic acid (EPA) converted in the body to ▼ *
AA (arachidonic acid)	Docosahexaenoic acid (DHA) In some algae

* this conversion is limited if there is a large intake of linoleic acid

Too much LA in the diet slows the conversion of alpha-linolenic acid to the long chain PUFAs. These long chain fatty acids are needed for the brain and eye development of infants and young children. The conversion process is also less efficient

● when there is excess trans fatty acids (TFAs)

● in the very young and old and

● following stress or viral infection

TFAs occur and the chemical structure of the molecule is altered when vegetable oils are heated as happens during the refining process and in the manufacture of margarine. There appears to be a link between high intakes of TFAs and some cancers. Try to use fats that are more stable when heated such as olive, groundnut and rapeseed oils.

Moreover try to include foods rich in LNA . Olive oil is a good choice as it is neither w-3 nor w-6 fatty acid so does not further upset the ratio between these two families. Flaxseed oil can be added to the diet from one year of age. Half a teaspoon of flaxseed (linseed) oil or one teaspoon of flaxseed powder or one teaspoon of canola (rapeseed) oil per day can help to achieve the right balance of essential fatty acids. The oil should not be heated and once opened, should be kept in the fridge. There are now vegan DHA supplements available that may be preferable. These are the long chain omega-3 fatty acids which come from algae.

Calcium
It is really quite safe to exclude dairy products from the diet and to maintain adequate calcium levels. However, it is important to ensure your child has a varied diet including calcium-containing foods. Different amounts of calcium are needed at different stages of life. Calcium is very important for growing bones and teeth and

Plant foods providing calcium			
Food group		**Amount**	**Calcium content (mg)**
Nuts	Almonds	6 whole (13g)	34
	Brazils	3 whole (10g)	17
	Hazelnuts	9 whole (10g)	14
Breads, cereals and potatoes	Wholemeal	Medium slice (36g)	19
	White	Medium slice (36g)	40
Seeds	Sesame seeds	1 tbspn (12g)	80
	Tahini	1 heapd tspn (19g)	129
Fruit	Figs	5 dried (100g)	250
	Raisins	1 tbspn (30g)	14
	Sultanas	1 tbspn (30g)	19
	Oranges	1 medium	50
	Olives	8 (20g)	12
	Apricots	5 dried (40g)	53
Vegetables (boiled)	Watercress	¼ bunch (20g)	34
	Spring greens	Medium portion (95g)	71
	Broccoli	Medium portion (85g)	34
	Okra	Medium portion (40g)	48
Beans and pulses (cooked)	Baked beans	1 small can (205g)	109
	Aduki beans	1 tbspn (35g)	14
	Chick peas	1 tbspn (35g)	16
	Lentils	1 tbspn (40g)	6
	Hummus	1 tbspn (30g)	12
Miscellaneous	Plamil White sun	100ml	42
	Provamel Alpro	100ml	84
	Granose	100ml	120
	Tofu	100g	510*

*if prepared with calcium sulphate

is also involved in the working of many systems in the body. Good sources of calcium include nuts and green leafy vegetables, fortified non-dairy milks, tofu made with calcium, blackstrap molasses, baked beans, textured vegetable protein and bread. Absorption from these foods has been shown to be excellent.

Calcium is widely distributed in foods of plant origin but meeting the Department of Health dietary reference values (DRV) using plant foods alone requires careful planning and calcium intakes in vegans are consistently lower. However, it has to be remembered that the DRVs are based on the omnivore population and it has to be questioned whether these recommendations are appropriate. For example, it may be that vegans have lower calcium needs than non-vegans because diets that are low in total protein and more alkaline have been shown to have a calcium sparing effect[3]. Therefore, perhaps it is not crucial that we consume large quantities of calcium but more important that our bodies are able to retain the calcium we consume.

The general omnivorous population consume too much protein which is linked to kidney disease and may adversely affect calcium balance. Studies have shown that excess dietary protein increases calcium excretion[4]. It also contributes to mineral loss from bone leading to osteoporosis This is because animal products are acidic and excess acidity in the blood disturbs mineral balance, including calcium. In contrast a vegan diet is more alkaline. Nevertheless, because calcium requirements of vegan children and adults have not been established it is recommended that parents aim to meet the Department of Health calcium requirements (see table below).

Department of Health calcium requirements	
Age	Calcium requirements mg/day
0-12 months	25
1-3 years	350
4-6 years	450
7-10 years	550
11-18 years women	800
11-18 years men	1000
19+ years	700

Calcium is well absorbed from many plant foods and vegan diets can provide adequate calcium if the diet regularly includes foods providing calcium (see table on previous page). In addition many new vegan foods are calcium fortified. About one pint (560ml) of soya infant formula per day will provide almost all the calcium needed by babies and toddlers up to three years. Moreover it should be kept in mind that bone mineral density is greatly influenced by weight bearing exercise. Physical activity is important at any age. Nowadays children lead a predominantly indoor life so lack of both physical activity and vitamin D could be key in a deterioration of bone health.

For good calcium status

● Consume calcium containing foods daily

● Ensure adequate vitamin D

● Avoid salt

● Increase physical activity, particularly weight bearing eg walking

Zinc

Infants require 4-7mg of zinc per day. Vegan infants have been shown to consume similar amounts of zinc to non-vegan children. However, zinc is less well absorbed from plant foods because the phytate content of plants interferes with zinc absorption[5]. Phytate is an anti-nutrient that can reduce the availability of minerals. Therefore, it is important to ensure good daily sources of zinc rich foods such as pulses, whole grains, wheat germ, fortified cereals, tofu and nuts. Fermented soya products such as tempeh and miso can improve zinc absorption[5]. If the diet is varied, vegan infants can easily meet the requirements for zinc. Sprouting is very effective in reducing phytate.

Vitamin D

There are few foods naturally containing vitamin D (vitamin D3, cholecalciferol) and all of these are animals products The main source of vitamin D is from sunlight. The skin can make all the vitamin D the body needs when it is exposed to gentle sunlight. Remember that children burn easily so don't expose them to direct sunlight. As little as half an hour playing outdoors two to three times per week is sufficient to meet your child's daily vitamin D requirements. The liver stores this vitamin to ensure an adequate supply through the winter months. Nevertheless it is prudent to ensure a regular intake of vitamin D fortified foods, particularly during the winter months and if living in more northerly areas. In addition, up to the age of five years the Department of Health recommend welfare drops which contain vitamin D (see page 34 for further information).

There is a vegan source of vitamin D (D2, ergocalciferol) and foods fortified with this vitamin include margarine, some non-dairy milks and fortified breakfast cereals. Vitamin D3 is not suitable for vegans and is made from fish oil or lanolin.

Vitamin B12

A one year old child needs 0.4mcg per day and this increases up to 1mcg per day at the age of ten years. It cannot be stressed enough how important it is that children take a reliable, daily source of this vitamin. It is available from fortified foods or in tablet and powder form. A variety of foods fortified with vitamin B12 are available including some brands of non-dairy milks eg Plamil White Sun or Provamel. Just 100ml of Plamil provides 1.6mcg, more than your infant's daily requirement. Other fortified foods containing this vitamin are TVP, yeast extracts and some breakfast cereals. Alternatively your child could take B12 in powder form which is palatable on its own or can be sprinkled on food.

Iron

A one to three year old child needs 1.9 mg per day. Iron intake must be ample to keep pace with a child's production of new blood. Iron deficiency anaemia is a common childhood nutritional problem no matter what the diet.[1] Although plant foods contain non-haem iron which is less well absorbed than the haem iron found in meat, iron is quite widely distributed in foods of plant origin and vegans tend to have higher intakes of this nutrient than non-vegans. Concerns have been expressed regarding the presence of anti-nutrients such as phytates that inhibit mineral and trace element absorption, particularly iron. However, iron absorption depends on the balance between dietary inhibitors (eg phytic acid) and enhancers of absorption such as vitamin C.

Vitamin C, which tends to be abundant in vegan diets, has been found to increase iron absorption, by up to 30% and more, when consumed with a meal[6]. Dairy products are a poor source of iron and they have an inhibitory effect on iron absorption[7]. Soya milk contains approximately seven times the amount of iron

as cow's milk but the bioavailability of iron from soya has been found to vary according to the level of phytates[8]. The iron in pea milk has been shown to be better absorbed than that from soya[9]. Good iron sources include whole or enriched grains and grain products, beans and lentils, nuts and seeds, green leafy vegetables, some breakfast cereals, tofu and dried fruit.

Foods	Amounts providing 2mg of iron
Lentils (boiled)	22g (0.8oz)
Sesame seeds/tahini	19g (0.7oz)
Blackcurrants (canned)	40g (1.4oz)
Black molasses	22g (0.8oz)
Figs (dried)	48g (1.7oz)
Raisins	53g (1.9oz)
Apricots (dried)	59g (2.1oz)
Iron fortified baby rice	30g (1oz)
Readybrek	15g (0.5oz)

Adapted from Vegan Nutrition by Gill Langley

Iodine

This mineral is responsible for producing thyroid hormones, which are important in the development of the nervous system, and for controlling metabolism. Concern has been raised about vegan diets that include foods such as soya beans and plants of the mustard family eg spinach and sweet potatoes, as they contain natural goitrogens that may cause thyroid deficiency. However, these foods have not been associated with thyroid insufficiency in healthy children, provided iodine intake is adequate. The most reliable vegan sources of iodine include sea vegetables, kelp tablets and Vecon yeast extract. However, don't overdo it as too much iodine can be as harmful as too little.

There is iodine in vegetables and grains but amounts vary according to the iodine content of the soil and recent studies suggest a low iodine concentrate in soil. Research suggests that the iodine intake of vegans may be rather low[10]. Therefore it is wise to include a reliable source of iodine two to three times a week.

Dietary Reference Values for Iodine mcg/day	
Age	Reference Nutrient Intake (RNI)
0-3 months (formula fed)	50
4-12 months	60
1-3 years	70
4-6 years	100
7-10 years	110
11-14 years	130
15-50+ years	150
Pregnancy – no increment	
Lactation – no increment	

The RNIs for infants are 50mcg/day rising to 70-130mcg/day for children and adolescents. The sea vegetable nori is very popular with children and is the most easily digested of the seaweeds. 7g of nori (about 3 sheets) will provide 100mcg and 1g of kelp can provide anything from 500mcg to 5000mcg. Try crumbling seaweed or a crushed kelp tablet into dishes two to three times a week.

Summary

■ Ensure your child has regular exposure to daylight. Vitamin D supplementation may be required if this is not possible

■ Include foods fortified with vitamin B12 and/or vitamin B12 supplements on a regular basis

■ Ensure a source of iodine two to three times per week

■ Make sure your child is getting adequate calories by including energy dense foods such as oils, seeds, nuts, dried fruits

■ Consuming fruits, rich in vitamin C, at each meal will assist iron uptake

■ Include calcium-containing foods or calcium fortified foods daily

■ Ensure a varied mixed diet

References for Chapter 6

1 Department of Health (1991) *Dietary Reference Values for Food Energy and Nutrients for the United Kingdom* Report of the Panel on DRVs on the Committee on Medical Aspects of Food Policy HMSO

2 Messina V Mangels AR (2001) *Considerations in planning vegan diets: Children* J Am Diet Assoc 101 661-669

3 Remer T Manz F (1994) *Estimation of the renal net acid excretion by adults consuming diets containing variable amounts of protein* Am J Clin Nutr 59 1356-1361

4 Barzel US Massey LK (1998) *Excess dietary protein can adversely affect bone* Journal of Nutrition 128 1051-3

5 Allen LH (1998) *Zinc and micronutrient supplements for children* Am J Clin Nutr 68 (suppl) 495S-498S

6 Hallberg L Brune M Rosslander L (1986) *Effect of ascorbic acid on iron absorption: mechanism of action and nutritional importance* Europ J Clin Nutr 46 317-27

7 Flynn A (1992) *Minerals and trace elements in milk* Adv Food Nutr Res 36 209-52

8 Hurrell RF Juillerat MA Reddy MB Lynch SR (1992) *Soy protein phytate and iron absorption in humans* Am J Clin Nutr 56 573-8

Jackson LS Kee K (1992) *The effect of dairy products on iron availability* Crit Rev Food Sci Nutr 31(4) 259-70

9 Davidsson L et al (2001) *Iron absorption from experimental infant formulas based on pea (pisum sativum) protein isolate: the effect of phytic acid and ascorbic acid* BJN 85 59-63

10 Key TJA Thorogood M Kennan J Long A (1992) *Raised thyroid stimulating hormone associated with kelp intake in British vegan men* J Hum Nut Diet 5 323-326

Lightowler HJ Davies GJ (1998) *Iodine intake and iodine deficiency in vegans as assessed by the duplicate portion technique and urinary iodine excretion* BJ Nutr 80 529-535

Krajcovicova-Kudlackova M Buckova K Klimes I Sebokova E (2003) *Iodine deficiency in vegetarians and vegans* Ann Nutr Metab Jan 1 47(5) 183-5

Problem solving

Getting children to eat vegetables can be difficult. In contrast, crisps, chocolates, chips and highly processed foods often attract the attention of youngsters. Marketing and peer pressure take their toll on the diet and health of young children and vegan infants are no exception to this. Therefore, as well as making foods healthy and nutritious, dishes need to be colourful and attractive, interesting and varied. Producing vegan dishes has never been easier with an ever increasing range of vegan burgers, sausages and other convenience products available. However try not to rely too heavily on convenience foods. There is a wide range of wonderful cook books available to experiment with.

DIFFICULT EATERS

It is worrying when your child seems to be eating irregularly or refuses to eat at mealtimes. Whether vegan or non-vegan, toddlers will take a stand on what they will and won't eat and providing a nutritious balanced diet can be quite a challenge. However, this behaviour is rarely harmful and unlikely to affect normal growth and development. Try not to get over anxious – children will eat when hungry and sometimes phases of poor eating are followed by 'catch up' eating. If your child is happy and growing then there is no need to worry. Here are a few tips which may help;

● Offer a variety of foods repeatedly - children's food preferences often change and it has been shown that offering foods repeatedly brings acceptance. What your child refused today may become tomorrow's favourite!

● Don't repeat the same food too often as this can make your child less willing to try something different

● Try not to give drinks just before a meal as this can spoil an appetite. It may encourage your child if you try new foods in the company of other children or when visiting family

● Novel foods can also be offered at picnics where everything is different. Try meals with different colours, shapes and textures. Use dishes with pictures so that the picture appears as the food is eaten. Vary meal locations, try a picnic in the garden

● Try different types of bread, cereal and pasta. Don't always stick to wholemeal and high fibre brands as they can be very filling for a toddler with a small stomach. Your child may prefer the texture of white bread occasionally which will do no harm

● Eat and drink something yourself, even if it is only a drink – this gives your toddler something to copy

● It has been shown that a new food can be offered up to 15 times before the child will try it. Persist for say 30 minutes and after this take the meal away without comment. Do not offer an alternative food or give the child anything extra to eat before the next meal time

● Eating should be fun and mealtimes a social occasion. Do not force your child to clear the plate or use one food as a reward for eating another

• Encourage regular meal patterns. Children with irregular meal patterns are more likely to have nutritionally unbalanced diets than those with set meal patterns. It is important a child learns appropriate feeding behaviour

• Get them involved – as children get older they can 'help' with food preparation by for example mixing ingredients in a large bowl, washing vegetables and using pastry cutters to cut out biscuit shapes

• Fill your cupboards with foods you want your child to eat, not foods that are laden with fats and sugars and set a good example by eating healthy foods too

• Commonly children go through a phase when they won't eat fruit and vegetables. It is often the texture they don't like so try stewing fruit and adding vegetable purees to soups and casseroles. Fruit juice can be used to supply the vitamins lost if whole fruit is refused

• Try buying baby size vegetables and fun size fruit

• Many children prefer finger foods or foods they can easily identify so stews, bolognaises and casseroles may not be too popular. Try to keep dishes simple

• Remember a healthy child when offered a variety of foods will not voluntarily starve. Most faddy phases will pass in a few months. However, if your child seems unwell or listless, persistently has no appetite or loses weight, consult your health care worker

Suggestions for ready to eat snacks for the food cupboard

Small packets of nuts and dried fruit
Fruit strips
Cereal bars
Ready to eat apricots and other dried fruit
Small cherry tomatoes
Plain popcorn
Soya drinks/yoghurts with added calcium
Nut and seed butters
Bread sticks and crackers
Bagels, rice cakes, chapattis and pitta breads

KEEPING YOUR CHILD WELL

Despite modern medicine, children are becoming more susceptible to disease. This is not surprising following the 1995 Department of Health survey which showed the typical diet of non-vegan children under five years of age was biscuits, white bread, sugary drinks, savoury snacks, chips and sweets[1]. Only half of these children ate any fruit at all and peas, carrots and potatoes were the only vegetables eaten by half of the children. In comparison, vegan children are introduced to a wider variety of unprocessed foods and, as shown by 'Parents' Experiences' in chapter 10, they eat well.

A healthy immune system comes from a healthy diet – young children will always get ill, even vegan children! So don't ever feel you have failed. We all feel as vegans we should be 110% healthy. A child's body has the most marvellous capacity for self-healing if it is given the right nourishment and care. Be assured that a vegan diet contains all the nourishment you and your child need.

Toddlers diarrhoea

This commonly occurs in children aged 10-20 months who are otherwise well, have a good appetite and growing normally. Undigested particles of food may be seen in the stools. Toddlers diarrhoea usually disappears by the age of 3 and the child comes to no harm. If there is no sign of an infection causing the diarrhoea, check that your child's diet isn't too high in fibre or she is not drinking too much fruit juice. If the diarrhoea continues seek medical advice.

MANUFACTURED FOODS

Many processed and packaged foods contain animal ingredients and these can be easily missed. If the amount of animal content is very small, labelling requirements do not require it to be declared on the ingredient list! For a full up-to-date list of suitable foods contact the Vegan Society (see appendix).

Listed below are some of the common animal derived ingredients you need to be aware of:

Milk derived products:
Casein/caseinates – milk proteins
Whey – by-product of the cheese making industry where it is separated from milk using rennet
Lactose – a sugar (disaccharide) found in milk margarines or fat spreads containing milk derivates

Egg products
Albumen – the protein in egg white

Other animal derived products
Rennet – an enzyme that comes from the lining of the stomachs of calves, generally used in cheese making or for making jellies
Gelatin(e) – derived from slaughterhouse waste such as animals bones, tendons, skins and ligaments. It is used as a thickening agent and frequently found in sweets and desserts
Shellac – a resin derived from insects. It is used to glaze fruit and sweets and to give a shiny finish to clothes and household items

Cochineal – a red dye that comes from female insects

FRUITARIAN AND RAW FOOD DIETS

A 100% raw food diet is not suitable for a growing child as it can contain too much fibre and may be low in protein. Infants have small stomachs and can easily be filled up before enough calories have been taken in. There is no evidence to support a fruitarian or raw food diet being nutritionally and reliably complete for vitamins and minerals, particularly vitamin B12. However, including a mixture of both raw and cooked food enables your child to eat a variety of foods and to provide the necessary micronutrients.

FIBRE

Concerns are often expressed that diets high in fruit and vegetables are also high in fibre and anti-nutrients which can adversely affect nutritional status. Excessive fibre can reduce the absorption of certain minerals such as calcium, zinc and iron. Nevertheless, although fibre intakes of vegan children are high compared with their peers, no disadvantages have been

reported. If food intake is low due to a child being full-up too soon, incorporating lower fibre foods is recommended such as refined grains, fruit juices, peeling fruit and vegetables and adding fat. Eating a wide variety of foods will not cause excess intake of fibre. Phytates, found in grains, seeds, nuts, vegetables and fruit, can inhibit iron absorption and may reduce the availability of calcium and zinc. Oxalate is a salt of oxalic acid, found in spinach, rhubarb and beetroot, and is viewed as an anti-nutrient because it interferes with the absorption of the essential minerals iron, magnesium and calcium. Nevertheless, the human digestive system is stimulated to reject anti-nutrients and the amount of oxalic acid and phytate in the diet can be adequately dealt with without any detriment to nutritional status. Also it is now known that if phytates and oxalates form a regular part of the diet, the body is able to adapt to their presence and partially counteract any negative effects on nutrient absorption. In addition, preparing foods in different ways can reduce the phytate content such as soaking beans prior to cooking and sprouting seeds, grains and pulses has a dramatic effect. There are many factors affecting the absorption of nutrients but few will alter the body's normal mineral status if a child is physically well and following a balanced diet.

REPLACING EGG AND DAIRY PRODUCTS

There is an ever increasing amount of vegan replacements on the market including milks, cheese, creams, yoghurts, ice creams and spreads. There are non dairy milks that are UHT or chilled, sweetened, fortified, GM free, organic or reduced fat. At least one non-dairy milk is now fortified with iodine; another is made from pea protein rather than soya. A range of spreads and cooking fats are available as alternatives to butter and dairy margarine and there are lots of new yoghurts, ice-creams, desserts and more. There is no lack of variety in following a dairy free diet. Alternatives to eggs include powdered egg replacements and tofu.

Many favourite non-vegan recipes can still be used and with a little adaptation and simple substitution, the end result can be the same! For example, for binding and thickening, thick vegetable stocks or mashed potato can be used. As a raising agent, baking powder or a mix of cider vinegar and bicarbonate of soda work. Talk to vegan friends for their ideas and tips. There are excellent vegan cookery books available - see the various cookery books available from The Vegan Society which often include lots of useful advice.

Summary

- Offer a variety of foods repeatedly

- If food intake is low cut down on high fibre foods

- Provide finger foods and foods that your child can easily identify

- Be assured a vegan diet can provide all the nourishment your child needs

References for chapter 7

1 Practice Nutrition (1995) Diet and health in pre-school children IBSN 0965-9722 Vol 4:2 July

Your child away from home

Away from the home, your child will constantly come into contact with sweets and various junk foods and may also be offered meat and other animal products. Parents may feel guilty keeping saying "no" to different foods. Taking the time to explain to your child why you are vegan and where food comes from will help her develop an appreciation and respect for food. The child can then choose whether she wishes to eat the animal based food or not. A few vegan parents have accepted that their child may choose to eat a non-vegan food when away from home. This is more often than not in order for the child to feel she fits in with her omnivore peers. It can cause a lot of heart searching and a couple of parents have addressed this in the case histories. However, it can be part of the child growing up. Frequently a child will return to a vegan lifestyle when she is older and more confident. Food and eating should be happy experiences.

Children (and adults!) will often be tempted by foods that are not good for our health such as crisps, sweets and take-aways. However, a small amount of such foods as part of healthy eating will not cause harm.

SWEETS AND TREATS
There are many mainstream sweets that are vegan and tempting to children. These include such things as Rowntrees jelly tots, Whizzers chocolate beans (vegan alternative to Smarties) and chocolate footballs, Vegebears' fruit jellies and liquorice, barley sticks, lollipops and vegan chocolate. There are some healthier alternatives such as fruit bars, small packs of dried fruits and cereal bars.

Many parents report that their children do not choose to eat as many junk foods and sweets as their omnivore peers. The secret is to offer alternative healthy foods as treats such as fruit, homemade cakes and biscuits, cereal bars and vegetable crisps.

PARTIES
Taking your child to a party can be seen as an opportunity to introduce other families to healthy foods. Many people may be unaware of the hidden sources of animal products so providing them with lists of foods and snacks that your child eats will help them to have a clear understanding. Also suggest common dishes that are eaten by omnivores too, like baked beans on toast, peanut butter sandwiches and potato waffles. You could share recipes and cook books – perhaps donate a cook book to your local playgroup or school!

If your child is setting off to a friend's party make sure that the hosts know your child follows a vegan diet. The chances are the party organizer may not be able to prepare special party foods in advance so it pays to prepare suitable foods for your child to take to the party.

If you are arranging your own child's party, there are lots of interesting 'party' foods available that are slightly healthier than the non-vegan equivalents. The following foods are popular choices for parties:

- Hot dogs/burgers
- Japanese rice crackers
- Sosmix rolls
- Savoury lentil slices
- 'Cheese' and pineapple/'sausages' on sticks
- Hummus on toasted fingers
- Popcorn
- Pizza
- Vegetable sticks and dips
- Water melon slices
- Home-made cakes and tarts such as flapjacks, date slices, apple cake
- Ice cream and jelly
- Figs, dates and other dried fruits
- Nori rolls

NURSERY/PLAYGROUPS

Make sure you discuss the vegan diet with your child's teacher. Often mid-morning or afternoon there will be a refreshment break. Check what the other children are having

(usually a drink and a biscuit) and provide your child with a carton of fruit juice or non-dairy drink with a biscuit. This will ensure your child doesn't feel different from her peers. If your child is staying for lunch you may prefer to provide a packed lunch – your child is unlikely to be alone as there are many cultural and health preferences and many parents prefer to supply their child's food.

LUNCH BOX IDEAS

If your child is attending playgroup or starting school, the following suggestions may be helpful in planning healthy but interesting lunch boxes. You will probably find other children will want to dip in and try your child's foods!

- Sandwiches and pitta breads filled with tofu, beansprouts and egg-free mayonnaise, mashed banana and apple, hummus and salad, yeast extract, tahini and peanut butter
- Rice or oat cakes topped with lentil pâté, peanut butter or nut pâté
- Nut and vegetable rissoles
- Thermos of soup
- Vegetable nori rolls
- Trail mix
- Carrot/celery sticks
- Tea breads, muffins and scones filled with jam or fruit spread
- Homemade fruit cake, flapjacks, oat slices
- Nut and cereal bars
- Soya yoghurts
- Mixed nuts and raisins and popcorn
- Encourage fruit consumption – kiwis, sharon fruit, fresh figs, dates and apricots in addition to the usual apples, oranges and bananas
- Fruit drinks and non-dairy milk shakes in cartons

Summary

- Take time to explain to your child where food comes from

- Share recipe and cook books with parents and teachers

- You will find other children (and parents too!) will want to try your food

What the experts say

PHYTOESTROGENS

The pros and cons of plant oestrogens, (phytoestrogens) have been debated and studies are often conflicting. Phytoestrogens are 'hormone'-like chemicals that naturally occur in many plants, seeds and grains. There are four main groups of phytoestrogens. Measuring the concentrations of phytoestrogens in food has proved difficult and reports on the content in foodstuffs have varied widely. Phytoestrogens can act in a similar way to the human hormone, oestradiol, but have a weak oestrogenic effect: 500-20,000 times less than oestrogens in the human body or the oestrogens in the contraceptive pill. Evaluating the health benefits of phytoestrogens is complex as these compounds have been shown to have both a positive and negative effect.

The Committee on Toxicity of Chemicals in Food produced a report in 2003 and concluded that "studies do not provide definitive evidence that phytoestrogens present in soya based infant formulae can adversely affect the health of infants"[1]. Furthermore, recent studies have demonstrated lower rates of coronary heart disease mortality in populations that consume soya, suggesting that phytoestrogens may have protective effects against cardiovascular disease. Indeed, recent research recommends adults should aim to consume 25g of soya protein daily to lower cholesterol.

IS SOYA SAFE FOR MY CHILD?

Yes. The nutritional benefits of soya are well documented. Soya is unique among beans because it contains all the eight essential amino acids and equivalent in protein quality to eggs, milk and meat. It is the richest source of vegetable protein and contains antioxidants which protect against disease. Soya contains omega-3 fatty acids and has been proven to lower cholesterol, a fat linked to heart disease and in addition has been shown to reduce cancer and improve kidney function.

Soya infant formulas can provide essential nutrients required for growth and normal development. They are manufactured to be safe and to meet the nutrition needs of babies aged four to six months (see pages 31-33 for further information on soya infant formula). Soya and other non-dairy milks can be included in an infant's diet at weaning, but should not be used as a sole feed for babies.

IMMUNISATION

Immunisation is such a huge topic and a small chapter in this book would not do it justice. For those parents requiring further information, there are a number of organisations giving the arguments against and the Department of Health official office giving the arguments for:

The Vaccine Information Service
PO Box 43
Hull HU1 1AA
Tel: 01482 562079
E mail: paddy@vaccinfo.karoo.co.uk
Web: www.vaccinfo.karoo.net
An information service about the fundamentals and flaws of vaccination, set up by parents to help other parents decide whether or not to vaccinate their children.

The National Vaccine Information Centre (VAN UK)
147 Bath Street
Ilkeston DE7 8AS
Tel: 0870 741 8415
E mail: enquiries@van.org.uk
www.van.org.uk
To assist parents with the difficult decision of whether or not to vaccinate their children and to make educated choices about vaccines and health care for their children.

Immunisation Programme (NHS)
Department of Health
Room 502A Skipton House
80 London Road
London
SE1 6LH
Call NHS Direct: 0845 4647
This is the official NHS vaccine information centre

The Informed Parent Co Ltd
Po Box 4481
Worthing
West Sussex BN11 2WH
Tel: 01903 212 969
www.informedparent.co.uk
Set up to seek information for parents regarding safety and effectiveness of immunisation

ORGANIC FOOD

"Organic" means that food is grown and processed using no synthetic fertilizers or pesticides. Over a lifetime, people will be exposed to many pesticides through their food, water and their environment. Individual foods can contain a mixture of pesticides. More and more people are purchasing organically grown and processed foods as a way to reduce their exposure to synthetic pesticides and fertilizers.

A Working Group for the Risk Assessment of Mixtures of Pesticides and Veterinary Medicines published a report in 2002 which concluded that the risk to people's health from mixtures of residues is likely to be small. It also said that children and pregnant or breast feeding women are unlikely to be more affected than most other people. The Food Standards Agency (FSA) published a draft action plan on the risk assessment of mixtures of pesticides in 2003 and has set up a research programme to look into the issue.

Controversially, the US Environmental Protection Agency suggests that infants and children may be especially sensitive to health risks posed by pesticides for several reasons

● Their internal organs are still developing and maturing

● In relation to their body weight, infants and children eat and drink more than adults, possibly increasing their exposure to pesticides in food and water

● Certain behaviours – such as playing on floors or lawns or putting objects in their mouths - increase a child's exposure to pesticides used in homes and gardens

The Agency believe that pesticides may harm a developing child by "blocking the absorption of important food nutrients necessary for normal healthy growth". The Agency goes on to explain that "if a child's excretory system is not fully developed, the body may not fully remove pesticides. Also, there are 'critical periods' in human development when exposure to a toxin can permanently alter the way an individual's biological system operates. Weight for weight, babies eat more fruit and vegetables, fruit juices and other pesticide containing foods than adult eaters so this needs to be borne in mind.

There is considerable interest in the health benefits of organically produced foods but unfortunately there have only been a few limited studies comparing the nutrient compositions of organically and conventionally produced crops[2]. Nevertheless the results are consistent in finding higher levels of nitrates and lower vitamin C concentrations in conventionally produced vegetables, particularly leafy vegetables and potatoes[3].

If buying non-organic fruits and vegetables, the FSA say it is not necessary to wash or peel fruit and vegetables in the UK because of pesticide residues. However, it is a good idea to wash them to ensure that they are clean and bacteria that might be on the outside are removed. Washing and peeling may help remove residues of certain pesticides but some pesticides are systemic which means they are found within the fruit or vegetable. Cooking the food can also reduce the levels of pesticides.

Imported food must comply with UK or EU legal limits on pesticide residues but if there aren't UK or EU legal limits for a particular substance, international standards are used. Residues are found in a slightly higher percentage of imported foods than in UK foods but the FSA report the levels found don't present a health risk. Remember, not eating any fruit and vegetables would be a much bigger risk to your child's health than eating foods containing low levels of pesticide residues! Nevertheless, for the health of children and the environment, if possible, try to buy organic foods as often as you can. However, remember organic foods are not fortified with vitamins and minerals.

VEGAN PARENTS

You've made it! It is said that nothing is worth getting unless you have had to work at it! It does take a lot of work and it is a challenge to create nutritious meals and snacks for your growing child. But straight away your child will reap the benefits. The following pages are written by vegan parents on how they've managed in bringing up their children on a vegan diet. We think our vegan children are a lot healthier and brighter than their omnivore peers – read for yourself from the testimonials in the final chapter.

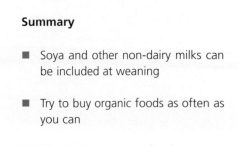

Summary

- Soya and other non-dairy milks can be included at weaning

- Try to buy organic foods as often as you can

- Remember organic foods are not fortified with vitamins and minerals

References for chapter 9

1 COT (2003) (Committee on toxicity of Chemicals in Food, Consumer Products & the Environment) *Phytoestrogens and health* The Food Standards Agency London

2 Williams CM (2002) *Nutritional quality of organic food: shades of grey or shades of green?* Proc Nutr Soc 61 (1) 19-24

3 Magkos F Arvaniti F Zampelas A (2003) *Organic food: nutritious food or food for thought?* A review of evidence Int J Food Sci Nutr 54 (5) 357-71

Parents' Experiences

Romy Morgan

When I was pregnant with Romy some people assumed I would begin eating meat again (which I hadn't done since I was 11) or at least drink some milk "for the good of the baby." Imagine their faces when I told them that, not only was I remaining vegan, the baby would be too! Naïvely I thought it would put their minds at rest when Romy turned out to be extremely tall and healthy. However, I have now realised that some people will never understand, so I don't let it worry me. Luckily I have an extremely supportive mother, best friend and husband (also vegan).

I worried that there might be a phase where Romy would try to eat non-vegan foods. I had visions of tantrums in supermarkets. It never happened. I have always been honest with her about where meat, dairy products and eggs come from so she has never wanted to eat them. I don't go into gory detail but she knows the facts. Romy had a 'fishless fishcake' the other day and I told her it tasted just like real fishcakes. She said very matter-of-factly "Yes, but you don't have to kill a fish to make it!"

Romy doesn't let her veganism get in the way of her life. She is just a normal four-and-a-half year old. She loves gymnastics; dancing; playing with Barbies; reading mountains of books, and being with her friends.

Romy is usually taken for a six-year-old, as she is so tall. She is also very forward. She sat unaided at four months; learnt the alphabet, colours and numbers at 18 months, and could read and write at three. So no worries about veganism affecting intellectual development then!

I breast-fed Romy for 16 months. She then weaned herself. We have been very lucky in that she has always enjoyed a wide variety of foods. Her favourites at the moment include, tofu (she pinches it before I've even started cooking); rice; curry; sandwiches with Tartex, soya cheese or peanut butter; fruit; vegetables; pasta; cereals and Yofu junior yoghurts. There actually isn't much she doesn't like.

I felt very pressured into having Romy immunised, against my better judgement. However, she was recently called for her pre-school MMR booster, which we are refusing. I feel much stronger after four years of parenting but it is hard feeling as though you are swimming against the tide of popular opinion.

Our families are now used to our different outlook. After hearing that Romy would be home educated, they hardly raised an eyebrow. It suits our relaxed lifestyle and we're happy. I would say to new vegan parents, read as much as you can to arm yourselves with the facts. If necessary, give literature to your Health Visitor or GP. My HV was brilliant. I knew what I was doing so she left me to it. She could see that Romy was thriving, so had no worries. Opposition from family can be harder to ignore but it wears off - either that or you get used to it! As long as you believe you're doing the right thing for your child, you'll keep your sanity. It can't be all that bad as we are now planning on doing it all over again and Romy can't wait to be a big sister!

Hazel and Colin Smithson

Mia and Matilda

Being a vegan parent is something that I have learnt to be; feeling my way, trying to adhere to my beliefs without becoming a tyrant. Like any other aspect of parenting, it is something that grows and develops as you learn more about your child and your own abilities as a parent.

When my first child went on to solid food, she seemed very fussy (something quite common to all children), and I considered resorting to raising her vegetarian. I felt quite isolated and I worried about her nutritional intake. But when I imagined myself feeding my daughter cheese, milk or eggs, I felt repulsed. So, I persevered. I am glad I did. My second child was a joy to feed: she ate up everything I gave her and by now I felt quite confident in my vegan parenting abilities!

Now, my eldest is five years old. She understands she is vegan, as are Mummy and Daddy, Grandma and Grandad and Aunty Sandra! She wears her veganism as a badge of honour. She has, however, tried dairy yoghurts and milk chocolate (at a friend's house). I explained to her that she could try them if she wanted (she was very insistent) but that they contained cow's milk and I wouldn't be buying them. I explained that whilst we were vegan at home, one day she would have to decide if she was going to stay

vegan. She thought about this then said "I think I will stay vegan, except for milk chocolate, because I like the taste!" I just laughed and said "OK darling". No doubt other vegan parents would disapprove of this approach but this is my way of doing it; just another aspect of the complicated business of being a parent.

Louise Blake

Matthew and Alice

I have been vegan myself for approximately ten years and vegetarian before that for as long as I can remember! When I discovered that I was pregnant with my first child, Matthew, I read every piece of information possible about bring up vegan infants. Plamil's Case Histories and Dr Klapper's book were particularly helpful. I wanted to embark on vegan parenthood as well informed as possible.

I breastfed Matthew for 18 months and my second child Alice for one year. Weaning my children was simple really because vegetable purees and the gradual introduction of cereals is recommended on 'conventional' diets too. My health visitors were always supportive but not particularly well informed unfortunately. It is a good job I didn't need any info from them! My main concern when they were babies was getting as much calorific value in the food and trying to reduce fibre intake. I used ground almonds in their cereal and extra virgin olive oil in their purees and they were always on the low side on the centile charts but I always argued that those charts were based on formula fed babies! When they were ready to give up the breast I introduced soya milk in cereal but they have never really been milk drinkers, which to me is the natural way.

Nowadays my children, now eight and four are still vegan and the picture of health. They are as faddy as the next child and will often refuse vegetables and fruit in favour of sweets and crisps. They prefer snacky food which I try to make as healthy as possible; for example hummus, pitta, breadsticks, fruit and sandwiches. We use all the meat and dairy alternatives such as Redwoods Cheatin' ham and cheese. A typical dinner for my children would be 'sausages', roast potatoes, a little veg or perhaps either cous cous or pasta with a burger. They do not really eat home cooked sauces or nutroasts which is a pity as I love cooking. Matthew loves homemade pies and I use Redwoods 'Chicken' chunks or Realeat Vegemince with my own pastry. They also love sausages and burgers.

I used to worry all the time about what they ate and if they would be healthy but now I relax a bit more because they have turned out so healthy and are rarely sick! My worries now are that they often feel left out when non-vegan food unexpectedly appears. I have given them the choice to eat vegetarian if they wish but they have both refused because they love animals so much. I always try to have alternatives ready but this is not always possible. Alice's playgroup is excellent and all the children cook vegan – I provide the ingredients for her other nursery.

Lisa Baxter

Carlin

In the first year bringing my son up on a vegan diet was perhaps the easiest part of being a first time new mum! I didn't really research much about vegan babies as it was clear to me prior to his birth that a vegan lifestyle was the spiritual, moral, ethical and healthy start that I wanted to give my child. I feel his birth was a wonderful gift of life and a small gift I was able to give him as a newborn was to nourish him without polluting such a pure and beautiful new soul with the dead flesh of animals.

As Sandra quite rightly points out in this book the foods we should ideally introduce babies to in their first important year are all naturally vegan – a fact I myself did not fully appreciate till I began learning on the job - what a pleasant surprise not having to look for alternatives! My biggest challenge was finding out I had a son allergic to sesame seeds, peanuts and all tree nuts, not to mention peas, lentils and the amazing chickpea! Did my resolve to continue his vegan diet falter? I would be lying if I said I didn't panic a bit - especially directly after the diagnosis with the sometimes pessimistic responses from many around me who were none too happy with his diet in the first place.

But I can truly say one year on I have a beautiful healthy little boy who has never eaten anything of animal origin and who has a better educated mother with regard to plant nutrition and the food industry in general. We no longer keep nuts in the house and in the last year I could probably count the amount of nuts and sesame seeds I have eaten in one hand - we do however enjoy a wide range of international vegan food, which is healthy and delicious - and that's coming from a vegan who used to eat blanched almond butter daily!

I found The Vegan Society helpful and they put me in touch with Sandra. My only regret is this book wasn't written sooner as the weaning section would have been something I could have referred to.

Audrey Bowman

Keith

He is very healthy. No coughs or colds this year at all which compared to his peers is amazing. He is one of the fittest in his school and excels at sport. I find it more and more incredible just how unhealthy some of his peers are – living on sweets, crisps, fried food and fizzy drinks.

Being vegan makes you aware of the importance of a well-balanced diet. I dread to think of the problems some kids will have in the future because they are being fed such an unhealthy diet. I am amazed at the number of times other parents say things like "Aren't you good", "I wish my child wouldn't eat so many junk foods" and "I wish my child ate what Keith eats". But it's in the hands of the parents – not the children! By the way, Keith is not deprived, he does occasionally eat sweets, chocolate, crisps, chips and a fizzy drink but he is not that bothered about them and rarely finishes them! The older Keith gets, the more convinced I am that his diet is giving him the very best start in life – what more can a parent do?

Sue Wilson

Joe

Joe was born in 1985, a healthy 7lb baby, delivered naturally after an easy pregnancy. He took quickly to breastfeeding and soon settled into a good routine. As a vegetarian from childhood and a vegan from my teens, naturally my baby would be introduced to a vegan diet. Joe enjoyed his food from the start. He began with single foods like rice and banana. I continued to breast feed him until he was seven months old, when he lost interest in breastmilk, I assume because he had become more interested in other foods available.

He went from breast to feeder cup, drinking juice that I made in a juice extractor, which was a must. His favourite was water melon but he also liked apple and pear. He loved pureed vegetables. I grew spinach, which is easy to grow. The leaves can be picked daily and cooked in minutes, providing loads of nutrients. He had this mixed with other vegetables, especially carrots and potatoes. I added ground nuts, cashews or almonds to fruit and he loved dried fruit like dates for finger foods.

For the sake of convenience Joe was introduced to dairy products at around ten years old but now, at 19 years of age, he is back on a vegan diet. Joe is fit and well and he rarely gets a cold.

Alison Salmon

Sorcha, Finn and Rory

In each pregnancy, I have been told to take, as a matter of course, iron supplements. Not because I am vegan (although vegan was written in big capital letters on my file by the consultants!) but because they are offered to all mums. I refused and when my blood results came back they showed perfectly normal levels of iron throughout my pregnancy.

I have breastfed all three children but with Sorcha I had problems during the first couple of weeks. I hadn't envisaged any problems and had not stocked up on soya formula. The midwives suggested formula but had no stocks of vegan formula – luckily I persisted in breastfeeding and things went ok but if I had needed formula it wouldn't have been available immediately.

Sorcha and Finn both went from breast milk to soya formula to enriched soya milk at age two with no problems at all. Rory went from breast milk to Plamil pea protein milk when he was 13 months. If I had known about the product before this then I would have put all my kids onto it as they have a lot of soya in their diet already and it provides a good balance.

My health visitor was new to her job when I had Sorcha and had never come across a vegan baby. She was very worried that she would not get the right nutritional requirements from the diet and suggested a referral to the dietitian at the local hospital. I refused saying there were no grounds for this as Sorcha was normal weight and that the vegan diet she was going to be weaned on to would be healthier than that of most of the population. In my experience, vegan mums know an awful lot more about nutrition and what is required for a healthy diet than most meat-eating parents.

We have had lots of pressure from our GP and Health Visitor to immunise the kids. None of the children have had immunisations as we feel that they don't work, are not vegan and the risks of vaccine damage too high. Sorcha and Finn have both been delisted from the local GP due to not having their MMR. The GP understands our point of view but because of the money involved will not have them on her register between the ages of two and five.

Sorcha takes a lunchbox to school as there are no vegan meals. It is similar to all her friends' lunches but vegan – 'cheese', peanut butter, hummus, rolls/sandwiches, fruit, soya dessert, chocolate or fruit/nut bar, pure fruit drink. Friends' parties don't cause too many problems as most foods can be substituted. I usually send a piece of cake or chocolate biscuit and some sandwiches. I'll even drop around a tub of Swedish Glace if the others are having ice cream just so they don't miss out. Party bags are often a problem but there are many 'mainstream' sweets that can be put into them.

Having non-vegan friends to lunch or tea has been no problem – most don't even notice that the cheese is vegan or the spaghetti bolognaise has no meat. I don't think I have had a child around who hasn't wanted more of the vegan ice cream.

One of the biggest helps for me has been having a couple of friends with vegan kids and also going to events where there have been vegan families – it gives you the reassurance that you are doing the right thing for your own kids.

Anne Cooper

David

David was born on 6th June 1972 of vegan parents. He was breastfed for about three months and at around one year old he looked fairly fat but soon returned to average for his age group. He progressed normally but until puberty he looked smaller than his contemporaries although just as full of energy. He did not have any innoculations and at four years old he caught Rubella (German Measles) whilst on holiday in Spain. For a day or two he was sleepy with a high temperature but soon recovered without any medication. Apart from winter colds, he has had no illnesses of note. He was always active, playing with his contemporaries and joining-in sports.

He stayed vegan at home but between ages 12 and 17 he took some dairy produce when outside the home. He became a committed vegan around age 18 and now has a vegan partner and children who are also vegan. In his later teens he shot up in height and is now around 5ft 11in with a well developed physique. He has always been keen on sports: weightlifting, windsurfing, cycling and triathlons.

He is a sociable person and gets on well with his working associates. He is now employed as an air pilot and has to submit to regular physical tests and always passes these without any problems.

Harry Mather

Both our children are happy, healthy, very fit and both doing well at school. Adam is in year four at school and is already year six equivalent! We are proud to be a vegan family!!

Sharon and Paul Cook

Adam and Amber

As vegan parents of two healthy children, now age seven (Amber) and nine (Adam), both vegan since conception, we have never encountered any worries or concerns about their vegan upbringing. It has been and still is positive and great!

Both children were born at healthy weights: Adam 8lbs 3oz and Amber 7lbs, even though I had smallish bumps on each pregnancy! I also had very small 32A breasts before pregnancy, but they grew whilst pregnant and produced lots of milk (and no you don't need to drink cow's milk or any other type of milk to produce human milk!), until I stopped breastfeeding the children at 14 and 15 months old. I ate only a little extra of what I fancied/what my body was 'telling' me, such as a second bowl of cereal with fortified soya milk each day, often in the afternoon, and I drank plenty of water! I never had iron deficiency in pregnancy and just took the occasional 'multi supplement for pregnancy' with folic acid. Both children were never sickly/positing/colicy babies and I never felt a natural need to 'wind' them!

Adam was not a fussy eater when he was a baby, or even now! However, Amber has never been great at trying new foods or eating lots, but she eats things from all her staple food groups which is the main thing!

Appendix

Appendix

RECOMMENDED BOOK LIST

- *Becoming Vegan** by B Davis & V Melina 2000 Book Publishing Co ISBN 1-57067-103-6

- *Plant Based Nutrition & Health** by Stephen Walsh 2003 The Vegan Society ISBN 0-907337-26-0

- *Raising Vegetarian Children** by J Stepaniak & V Melina 2003 Contemporary Books

- *Vegan Nutrition* by Gill Langley 1988 The Vegan Society ISBN 0-907337-18-X

- *Pregnancy children and the vegan diet* by Michael Klaper MD 1978 Gentle World Inc PO Box 1418 Umatilla Florida 32784 available from The Vegan Society

- *Food Allergy Survival Guide (2004)** by Vesanto Melina, J Sephaniak and Dina Aronson. Healthy Living Publications

*available from The Vegan Society

RECIPES

There are lots of first foods that you can experiment with - here are just a few suggestions!

FIRST FOODS
(AFTER 17 WEEKS)

Baby rice – choose those fortified with additional iron and B vitamins. Make up as directed on the packet

Fruit purée (apple, pear, ripe melon, peach, mango)
Tinned fruit in natural juice can also be pureed. Avoid fruit with seeds or pips unless you can remove them first. Peel if appropriate and simmer in a little water until tender. Liquidise or sieve using a little cooking fluid if necessary

Banana purée (or avocado or ripe melon)
Choose very ripe fruit. Peel and mash thoroughly. Add a little cooled boiled water if necessary to make a soft consistency

Rice and apple pudding
60g (2oz) apple, peeled and cored
15g (1/2 oz) ground rice

Stew apple in water until soft. Sprinkle in ground rice and cook over a low heat. Cook for 2-3 minutes, stirring continuously until thickened. Add baby's usual milk

Pumpkin or courgette purée
Peel the pumpkin and remove seeds. Cut off the ends of the courgette. Cut into small pieces and cook in boiling water until tender. Purée

Carrot purée
250g (8oz) carrots, peeled and chopped
2 tbspn baby rice
6 tbspns baby's usual milk

Steam carrots or place in boiling water, cover and simmer and cook until soft. Blend the vegetables to a purée with 4 tbspns of the cooking liquid. Mix the baby rice and milk together, add to the vegetables and stir until well mixed.

Spinach purée
Remove stems and wash thoroughly. Cook in a little water until tender. Purée. Do not give more than twice a week as the oxalic acid content affects the body's absorption of some nutrients

Swede/parsnip and carrot purée
(2-3 servings)
120g (4oz) chopped swede/parsnip
120g (4oz) chopped carrot

Put the ingredients in a saucepan and bring to the boil. Cover and simmer until the vegetables are soft. Remove from the heat and purée in a liquidiser or push through a sieve to get a smooth consistency. Mix with baby's usual milk

STAGE TWO (AFTER SIX MONTHS)

Apricot or date purée
Soak dried fruit overnight. Drain and simmer in a little water until tender. Liquidise or sieve using a little cooking fluid if necessary. Note: can have a laxative effect

Lentil or rice with vegetables
30g (1oz) rice or red split lentils
60g (2oz) turnip
60g (2oz) potato
5 fl oz (150ml) soya formula or non-dairy milk

Simmer all the ingredients in a saucepan until soft. Liquidise to a smooth consistency

Tofu smoothie
Silken tofu and fruit of choice
Blend and serve

Lentil purée
(1 serving)
½ small onion, finely chopped
1 small carrot, finely chopped
25g (1oz) split red lentils
5 fl oz (150ml) water

Gently cook the onion carrot and lentils in the water until soft. Sieve, thinning with a little water as necessary.

Savoury lentils
(3-4 servings)
150g (5oz) potatoes
150g (5oz) carrots
15g (5oz) cooking apples
90g (3oz) red or green lentils
330ml (11fl oz) water
150g (5oz) cauliflower
30g (1oz) margarine

Peel and chop the vegetables, peel and core the apple and bring to the boil with the lentils in the water. Cover and simmer for 30 minutes. Add the cauliflower and cook for a further 15 minutes. Blend thoroughly. Simmer until soft, add margarine and serve.

Pancakes

(makes 12 x 4" pancakes)
300g flour (mix of wholemeal and unbleached white)
2 tspns baking powder
3 tbspns ground flaxseeds
2 tbspns rapeseed oil
500ml non-dairy milk

Mix the dry ingredients and make a well in the centre. Add the oil and milk and stir thoroughly. Cook in a lightly oiled pan for 2-3 minutes on each side.

Biscuits

(makes 12)
1½ tbspns flaxseeds
125ml warm water
60 ml oil
250 ml milk
75g (3oz) wholemeal flour
2 tspns baking powder

Blend the flaxseeds, water, oil and milk until creamy. Add the flour and baking powder and make into a dough. Roll out ¼" thick onto a floured surface. Cut into biscuits and bake for 12 minutes 190°C/Gas Mark 5/375°F

STAGE THREE (8-12 MONTHS)

Smooth nut and seed butters can be introduced after 8 months but if there is a history of allergy, delay introducing until the child is 3 years of age.

Muesli*

(1 serving)
1 pear, peeled and chopped
5 dried apricots, simmered in a little water until soft
150ml fortified non-dairy milk
15g (1/2 oz) oats

Place oats and milk in saucepan. Simmer for 3-4 minutes or until mixture thickens. Cool a little and place in a blender with cooked apricots and pear chunks. Blend until smooth and creamy

Hummus

Any of the supermarket or health food shop own brands will be suitable. However, hummus is very cheap and relatively easy to make yourself.
1 x 425g can of chickpeas
1 clove garlic, crushed
2 tbspn tahini
1 tbspn flaxseed oil
1 tbspn lemon juice

Drain the chickpeas and put the liquid aside. Put all the ingredients into a blender with 3 tablespoons of the reserved liquid. Blend until smooth, adding more of the liquid as necessary.

Pâté

4oz (100g) millet
3 tbspns oil
2oz (40g) ground brazils
2oz (50g) ground sunflower seeds
1 small onion, grated
1 dessertspoon yeast extract
1 tspn dried sage
2oz (50g) sesame seeds
2oz (50g) soya flour

Cook the millet in 1pt (20 fl oz) water until mushy, adding more water if necessary. Add all the ingredients and put into an oven dish and bake at Gas Mark 4/350°F/180°C for 30-40 minutes

Potato tofu casserole
(4 servings)
125g (4oz) mashed potato (with margarine and non-dairy milk)
250g (8oz) tofu mashed
1 teaspoon fresh parsley
1 tbspn oil
1 small onion grated (optional)

Sauté onion in the oil and mix in potato and tofu. Mix well together and spread into oiled tin and bake for 30 minutes. Serve with steamed vegetables

Nori rolls
(4 servings)
4 large sheets of dried nori
2oz (50g) rice
1 medium carrot diced
3 tbspns peas
1 spring onion chopped
2oz (50g) grated soya cheese

Cook the rice in boiling water but 5 minutes before it is ready, add the diced carrot and cook for 5 minutes. Add the peas and onion and bring to the boil, then drain off any remaining water. Remove from the heat and add the grated cheese. Spread it on to the sheets of seaweed, moisten the edges with water and roll up. Cut each roll into 4 pieces. Ideal for parties and picnics. Use other popular fillings such as tofu and avocado, beans and sweet potatoes, sweetcorn, rice and nuts.

Sweet potato bake
(4 servings)
390g(13oz) sweet potato, peeled and chopped
360g(12oz) tinned beans
180g (6oz) leeks, finely chopped
90g (3oz) chopped tomatoes
1 tspn dried herbs
30g (1oz) margarine

Melt the margarine and add the leeks and potatoes and sauté for 8-10 minutes. Add the tomatoes and enough water to cover. Bring to the boil and add the beans. Place in a casserole dish and cook in the oven, Gas mark 4, 350°F, 180°C for 25 minutes. Add the mixed herbs and cook for a further 5 minutes.

Nectarine and apple fool
(2-3 servings)
2 apples
2 nectarines
1 small pot of yoghurt
1 banana

Peel and slice the fruit and place in a pan with 100 ml of water. Simmer until soft. Chill for half an hour, then stir in yoghurt and decorate with sliced banana.

Baby's first casserole*
(1-2 servings)
1 small onion, finely chopped
1 medium carrot, diced
1 medium potato, diced
75g (3oz) red lentils
1 tsp mixed dried herbs
50g (2oz) tinned peas or beans
400ml vegetable stock
1-2 tbspn vegetable oil for frying

Fry the onion in a little vegetable oil until tender. Add the remaining ingredients and place in a casserole dish with lid. Place in a preheated oven at 180°C, 350°F or gas mark 4 for approx 1 hour or until cooked. Cool a little before blending

*Recipes provided by The Vegan Society

STAGE FOUR (OVER ONE YEAR)
You can now introduce your child to your meals. We have not included any recipes in this section because any meal for adults can be adapted for a child. There are lots of excellent vegan cookery books available from The Vegan Society that will suit all tastes. For meal suggestions, see menu ideas on page 52.

USEFUL ADDRESSES

ALLERGY INFORMATION
Allergy UK – British Allergy Foundation
3 White Oak Square
London Road
Swanley
Kent
BR8 7AG
www.allergyuk.org
Tel: 01322 619864
Provides information, advice and support to help with managing all allergic conditions

BREASTFEEDING SUPPORT
Association of Breastfeeding Mothers
PO Box 207
Bridgwater
Somerset
TA6 7YT
www.abm.me.uk
Tel: 0870 401 7711
Voluntary group founded by mothers experienced in breastfeeding counselling

La Leche League
PO Box 29
West Bridgford
Nottingham
NG2 7ND
www.laleche.org.uk
E-mail: llgb@wsds.co.uk
Tel: 0845 120 2918
Helping mothers to breastfeed through mother-to-mother support, encouragement, information and education

The National Childbirth Trust
Alexandra House
Oldham Terrace
London W3 6NH
www.nctpregnancyandbabycare.com
E-mail: enquiries@national-childbirth-trust.co.uk
Tel: 0870 444 8707
Breastfeeding helpline: 0870 444 8708
Offers support in pregnancy, childbirth and early parenthood

IMMUNISATION
(see chapter 9)

VEGAN SOCIETY
The Vegan Families List
The Vegan Society holds a list of vegan families in the UK which is available free on receipt of a stamped addressed envelope. This is a network of vegan families who have or have had vegan children and are happy to be contacted for advice and support. If you would like your family to be added to the list, please send a SAE for a vegan families questionnaire.

The Vegan Society
Donald Watson House
7 Battle Road
St Leonards on Sea
East Sussex
TN37 7AA
Tel: 01424 427393
Fax 01424 717064
www.vegansociety.com
E-mail: info@vegansociety.com

OTHER ORGANISATIONS
Animal Aid
The Old Chapel
Bradford Street
Tonbridge
Kent
TN9 1AW
Tel: 01732 364546
Fax: 01732 366533
Web: www.animalaid.org.uk
E-mail: info@animalaid.org.uk
Animal Aid is the largest UK animal rights group which campaigns peacefully against all forms of animal abuse and promotes a cruelty free lifestyle

The Vegetarian Society
Parkdale
Dunham Road
Altrincham
Cheshire
WA14 4QG
Tel: 0161 925 2000
Fax 0161 926 9182
www.vegsoc.org
E-mail: info@vegsoc.org

Vegan Views
Flat A15
20 Dean Park Road
Bournemouth
BH1 1JB
E-mail: info@veganviews.org.uk
Website: www.veganviews.org.uk
An independent journal published quarterly by vegans for vegans. Relying on contributions from members with letters, articles, news and events. It realises that many vegans feel isolated from society and appreciate contact with and news and opinions of other vegans.

Index

Index

Notes

Notes

Notes

NO MORE PEERING AT INGREDIENTS LISTS OR TEARING YOUR HAIR OUT TRYING TO FIND VEGAN PRODUCTS!

An indispensable guide to all things vegan, the *Animal Free Shopper* is a must-have for vegans, vegetarians and the lactose intolerant.

With over 15,000 products listed, ranging from food and drink to toiletries and cosmetics, and including a section of products for babies & infants, this handy pocket-sized guide takes the stress out of vegan shopping.

To order your copy today, visit www.vegansociety.com/shop or call 01424 448832

LOOKING FOR A VEGAN MULTIVITAMIN?

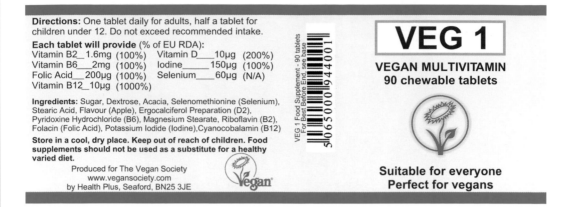

Directions: One tablet daily for adults, half a tablet for children under 12. Do not exceed recommended intake.

Each tablet will provide (% of EU RDA):

Vitamin B2	1.6mg	(100%)	
Vitamin B6	2mg	(100%)	
Folic Acid	200µg	(100%)	
Vitamin B12	10µg	(1000%)	
Vitamin D	10µg	(200%)	
Iodine	150µg	(100%)	
Selenium	60µg	(N/A)	

Ingredients: Sugar, Dextrose, Acacia, Selenomethionine (Selenium), Stearic Acid, Flavour (Apple), Ergocalciferol Preparation (D2), Pyridoxine Hydrochloride (B6), Magnesium Stearate, Riboflavin (B2), Folacin (Folic Acid), Potassium Iodide (Iodine),Cyanocobalamin (B12)

Store in a cool, dry place. Keep out of reach of children. Food supplements should not be used as a substitute for a healthy varied diet.

Produced for The Vegan Society
www.vegansociety.com
by Health Plus, Seaford, BN25 3JE

VEG 1 Food Supplement - 90 tablets
For Best Before End: see base

VEG 1

VEGAN MULTIVITAMIN
90 chewable tablets

Suitable for everyone
Perfect for vegans

THEN VEG 1 COULD BE THE ONE FOR YOU!

Specially formulated for The Vegan Society, VEG 1 contains vitamin B12, vitamin D, iodine and selenium as well as vitamins B2, B6 and folic acid - making it the perfect addition to a healthy vegan diet for people of all ages.

One tablet per day meets the needs of adults and teenagers while one every other day (or half a tablet each day) meets the needs of younger children.

A very small amount of sugar (about half a gram per tablet) and apple flavour have been included to make the tablets palatable and chewable, which should make persuading children to take them a lot easier.

The tablets can be purchased direct from the Vegan Society at just £4.99 plus p&p for three months adult supply (90 tablets).

See www.vegansociety.com/shop or call 01424 448832

Vegan Passport – 2nd Edition
ISBN: 0-907337-30-9
Cover Price: £3.99

The new and expanded *Vegan Passport* now boasts 56 languages, accounting for an incredible 93% of the world's population. Slip it into your pocket, and you'll find that wherever your travels take you, you'll have no problem explaining your dietary needs (also handy for clarifying your needs when visiting restaurants in the UK). And if you do find somewhere where none of the 56 languages apply, the fail-safe pictures from the previous edition have been retained. It's never been easier to travel the world without compromising on your vegetarian or vegan diet.

See www.vegansociety.com/shop or call 01424 448832

Membership / Renewal

THE Vegan SOCIETY

○ I wish to become a member and support the work of the Vegan Society.

○ I wish to renew my membership.
Membership No. (if known)...

Name:..Address:..

....

Postcode:.................................Tel:....................................email:............................

Date of Birth: (for security purposes)........./........../..........Occupation:.........................

○ Please tick this box if you are a dietary Vegan.
This entitles you to voting rights in the Society's elections if aged 18+.

○ Please treat any membership subscription or donation since 6th April 2000 as Gift Aid. I have paid UK income or capital gains tax equal to the amount the Society reclaims.

○ My income is less than £8000 per year and I qualify for the low income discount of 33%.*

○ I wish to enrol other members of my household for an additional £7 each.**

A copy of the Society's rules (Memo & Articles of Association) can be viewed on our website or at our office. Alternatively you may buy a copy for £5.

Please give full names of additional members and specify if dietary vegan and / or under 18. (If more than four additional members please attach separate sheet.)

Membership

Individual **£21**	
* Minus **£7** low-income deduction (if applicable)	
** Add **£7** per additional household member	
Life **£350**	
Memo & Articles of Association **£5**	
Overseas: Europe +**£5** / Rest of World +**£7**	
Donation	
Total:	

How to pay

Cheque / PO payable to *The Vegan Society*

Credit / Debit card (see overleaf)

Direct Debit (ring for details)

Website: www.vegansociety.com

Payment must be made by credit card, sterling International money Order or sterling cheque drawn on a British bank.

○ Please debit my Visa / Mastercard / Access / Eurocard / Visa Delta / Connect / Switch / Solo card number

Name on card:...Signature:...

Today's date........./........./.......Start date:........./........Expiry date......../........Switch Issue No.:....................

Please send to: **The Vegan Society** ¦ **Donald Watson House** ¦ **7 Battle Road** ¦ **St Leonards on Sea** ¦ **East Sussex** **TN37 7AA** ¦ **UK**
Tel: **01424 448832** ¦ Fax: **01424 717064** ¦ Visit: **www.vegansociety.com** ¦ email: **membership@vegansociety.com**

JOIN

THE

Vegan

SOCIETY

The Vegan Society promotes ways of living free from animal products for the benefit of people, animals and the environment.

We publish a range of resources all aimed at educating people about the benefits of veganism and supporting those who have already made the transition to a vegan diet.

By joining us, you have access to the most comprehensive information on all aspects of veganism, and you support the Society's work helping more people to go vegan and encouraging manufacturers, caterers and healthcare professionals to provide improved services for those choosing to follow an animal-free lifestyle.

To join or request more information, call us on *01424 427393* visit *www.vegansociety.com/shop* or fill in the form overleaf